Helen Hardin, a Pueblo, is the star. Her work is complex, nuanced, strange; soft metallic colors and unexpected angles seem to dance together in half-traditional designs. Paradoxically her art seems both old and new.

—PAUL RICHARD
The Washington Post
(August 23, 1980)

CHANGING WOMAN

The Life and Art of Helen Hardin

JAY SCOTT

Northland Publishing

To Birdie and Gene

Text copyright © 1989 by Jay Scott
Photographs copyright © 1989 by Cradoc Bagshaw
All Rights Reserved.

FIRST EDITION, 1989
FIRST SOFTCOVER EDITION, 1993

ISBN 0-87358-489-9 (hardcover)
ISBN 0-87358-567-4 (softcover)
Library of Congress Catalog Card Number 89-42662
Composed in the United States of America
Printed in Hong Kong by Dai Nippon
Designed by David Jenney
Softcover Cover Designed by Rudy J. Ramos

Library of Congress Cataloging-in-Publication Data

Scott, Jay.
    Changing woman : the life and
      art of Helen Hardin/by Jay Scott
    ISBN 0-87358-489-9 (hardcover)
    ISBN 0-87358-567-4 (softcover)
    1. Hardin, Helen, 1943-1984.
    2. Artists—United States—
    Biography. I. Title.
N6537.H347S28 1989
759.13—dc20
[B]   89-42662

Front Cover: *Changing Woman,* acrylic, 1981
Photograph copyright © 1989 by Cradoc Bagshaw

0468/5M/7-93

Contents

Prologue   A Dance Not Easily Done

The spirit people in Helen Hardin's paintings are people who have been pieced together. Sometimes the pieces fit harmoniously; more often than not, each section of a Helen Hardin image is in opposition to its neighbors. When I first met Hardin at her middle-class condominium across from St. Joseph's Hospital in what, until urban renewal, had been one of Albuquerque's notoriously poor *barrios,* Martineztown, there was nothing to indicate that the roots of the art might be found in the artist. The Helen Hardin persona seemed all of a piece—and the superficial image of a successful, photogenic, intelligent painter of Native American extraction was a pretty picture indeed.

My involvement with Hardin came about, or so I thought, simply. Years before, I had grown up in Albuquerque, and had first worked as a serious journalist there. I covered Indian affairs, movies and occasionally art, for the *Albuquerque Journal.* In 1975, I moved to Canada and stayed, returning home often to visit relatives and friends. On one of those visits, in the early eighties, I saw one of Hardin's older paintings, *Lost Fertility Regained* (1974), at an Albuquerque gallery and purchased it without a second thought. (The price was modest enough to qualify as ridiculous.) Long after I had gone back to Toronto and had gone back to work (as a critic for *The Globe & Mail,* Canada's national newspaper, and a contributing editor for *Canadian Art*), I found myself increasingly fascinated by the artist, about whom I knew little except that she was the daughter of Pablita Velarde, an even more famous Southwest painter, and by her art, about which—based on this one picture and reproductions of additional work I found in books—I thought I knew a great deal: most particularly that, along with James Havard, Fritz Scholder and a few others, she was at the cutting edge of Indian-influenced American art.

I arranged an interview with her, returned to Albuquerque, and was entertained by a 5′ 2″ woman in jeans and a paint-spattered top. She offered white wine, drank a little herself, and excused herself at

Lost Fertility Regained, 1974

one point to turn off the soap opera that was blaring in her studio at the rear of her home. She was enthusiastic but realistic about her own work ("I can't do a masterpiece every time I sit down to paint"), highly critical of the work of others (she thought Picasso over-rated, Scholder "burned out"), contemptuous of the politics of many Indian organizations (everything from the Bureau of Indian Affairs to the American Indian Movement earned her scorn) and even critical of her own people ("Indians feel too sorry for themselves"). But when she talked of Indians or whites, she talked of them as individuals, not as groups; being defined as part of a group — of any group — obviously bothered her. Only later would I realize that not being defined as part of a group bothered her even more: her independent stance, culturally correct for a professional woman in the eighties, originated as defense against another, far older culture that had rejected her.

Words such as contempt and scorn do not communicate the blithe spirit with which Hardin delivered her diatribes. She laughed easily of her reputation as "a bitch," admitted she thought there was truth to the allegation ("I've stirred up a lot of trouble"), tended to dismiss her pain ("I've had my problems, who hasn't?") and lost her sense of humor only once, when I asked her about her famous mother. "Are you going to write about her, or is the article about me?" she wondered. I didn't know, then, that the emotional subtext of that question was bottomless: I didn't know that she was an abused child, and that she harbored an especially acute case of the characteristic ambivalence of the child who has been damaged. On the one hand, she hated and wanted to dismiss the abusive parent; on the other, that parent would always wield over her an extraordinary power, the power of love withheld.

Assuming no more than that Hardin was rightly concerned that I might be wasting her time if my interest was in reality with her mother, I confessed that although I had grown up with and had enjoyed the well-known "earth paintings" of Pablita Velarde, I thought them a peculiar part of the history of Southwest cultural anthropology. I saw them less as art than as ultimately depressing

Carriers of the Father Universe, 1974

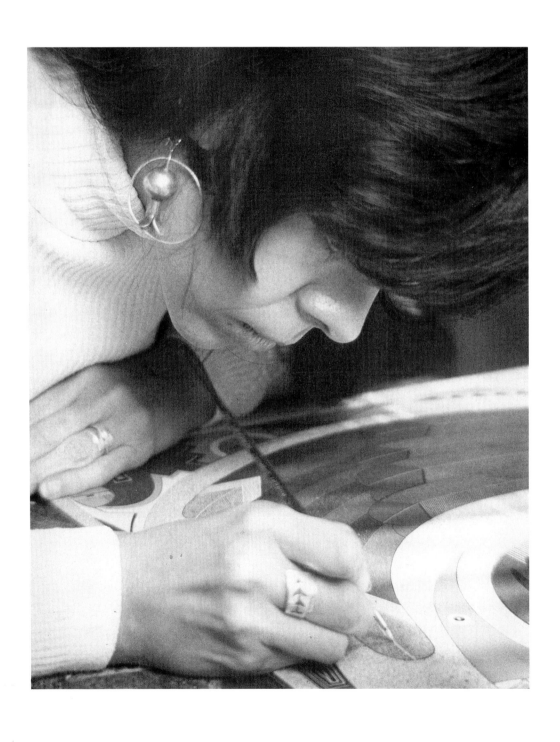

exhibits in the spiritual colonialization of the Indian people. Hardin's art, though obviously drawing on her Indian tradition, seemed to be very much in the mainstream of the modern European and North American aesthetic project, which is to say, very much concerned with the search for self.

It was the right answer. How right, I didn't know—I had been worried that I was perhaps too frank, had perhaps insulted her mother. Not so. Hardin immediately relaxed. Smiled. I had already told her I did not admire the popular and prolific artist R.C. Gorman, and now I had told her that I was not overly impressed with her mother. I was on the side of the good guys: I shared her opinion of the bad guys. "It was important to Helen," her husband Cradoc Bagshaw would tell me after she had died, "that people dislike the people she disliked. But she *did* know that some of her hatreds were unreasonable. She had an unreasonable hatred of fat women with kids in the grocery store; partly that may have been because that was what she was afraid she might become. And she refused to acknowledge the existence of the Internal Revenue Service, so three years later, we'd pay penalties. Helen simply couldn't deal with people she thought were stupid and she generalized incredibly as to who was stupid—anyone who worked for a utility company, or anyone who worked for the IRS."

When Helen Hardin worked, her concentration was intense and sometimes isolated her. "When she painted, she was gone," her husband, Cradoc Bagshaw, recalled.

Or anyone who valued her mother's work above hers. I would learn that as Hardin was growing up, Pablita Velarde had placed her career above the demands of her family, especially the demands of the daughter who evinced a desire to also become an artist. Hardin never recovered from her mother's coldness, and predictably resolved never to treat her own family in the same way. It was a resolve she was not able always to keep, but it was a resolve she never forgot. "When she painted," her husband remembered, "she was gone. She just wasn't there. She'd come down and visit us every once in a while, but where she lived was really in her paintings, and where that was…well, she wasn't really comfortable in this world. She retreated into Indian spirituality when she painted, a spirituality that she had been denied direct access to by her own people. During the twelve years we were together, I never understood fully what she was up to; I only understood after she died. But when she would come down, or come back, and spend time with me and her daughter, Margarete, she was here fully for us. For as long as she could stand to be here."

That day we met in Albuquerque, Hardin responded to my speech about her mother's art with a smile, yes, but it was followed by a terse comment. "You didn't always think so," she said. And smiled again. I pleaded ignorance. "More than ten years ago, when you lived here, you covered the New Mexico Arts and Crafts Fair for the *Albuquerque Journal*," she reminded me (I had said nothing about an Albuquerque connection, and was planning to publish the interview with her only in *The Globe & Mail*), "and you came by my mother's booth and my booth. You wrote about her, but you never wrote about me. Not once in the three years you covered the Arts and Crafts Fair did you ever even mention me." She was right: and what's more, to this day, I have no recollection of ever having seen her work before I happened upon *Lost Fertility Regained* in that Albuquerque art gallery years later. When I left her condominium that day, I think that in an innocent sense, I had fallen in love: I was transfixed by her honesty, by her inability to let sleeping dogs snore. All her life, Helen Hardin made things more difficult for herself than they might reasonably have needed to be, but she did so because she could not silence an inner voice that demanded that the truth, as she saw it, be served. Her friend, the Indian painter John Nieto, put it as well as anyone ever has:

"Helen was right on the edge of everything. She went to Indian Market in Santa Fe, which she had outgrown as an artist, longer than she needed to—much longer than she should have—because she couldn't give up what she saw as her heritage. At the same time, she wanted success in New York, and not as an 'Indian woman painter.' Then, she married a white man, which put her on another kind of edge. Whites feel one way about that, but Helen marrying a white man really put it over the line for Indians. For an Indian man to marry a white woman, to make her his 'squaw,' is accepted, it's not a huge problem, but an Indian woman marrying a white man is *anathema* to Indian men, and even Indian women. Helen probably had the strength to do so many of these things because she was not really a 'reservation Indian.' For reservation Indians, dealing with the experience of what it actually means to be an Indian is too painful, which is why I think there are very few famous Indian artists, and even fewer who are any good. Instead of dealing with their pain—with their lives—in their art, most of them deal...with a tourist's idea of Indian imagery and spirituality. But Helen dealt with the real thing. Even when it meant remembering the heritage they tried to take away from her. Even when it caused her hurt."

Hardin's husband would sometimes ask her, in the first years of their marriage, what on earth had happened between her and her people, and how she felt about it. "The only thing I could ever get out of her was, 'I hurt.'"

John Nieto said, "She was doing a dance not easily done."

ONE
Everything Tries To Be Round

In January of 1981, Helen Hardin entered her studio and began a new acrylic. Like much of her previous work, the painting was to be of a face; like many of her previous faces, it would be drastically stylized; like nearly all of her previous faces, it would exist in a fantastic netherworld, a mythological universe poised precariously between the human and the inhuman, the sacred and the profane, the godlike and the demonic, the sublime and the primal. The features were contained within a perfect circle, a Jungian archetype of psychic wholeness and the symbol for Hardin of life itself, but everything else about the painting was fragmented, jagged and asymmetrical. The masklike face was incorporeal: the eyes and mouth floated in the foreground over airbrushed rectangles that intersected with other rectangles to form a pattern that could almost be called a plaid. The face was bisectional: the angry orange- and red-rimmed bull's eye on the left was the natural accompaniment to the mouth on the same side, a rectangle filled with fangs, just as the sleepy eye on the right, a rectangle filled with rectangles, was an apposite companion to the mouth, a benign pucker fashioned from concentric circles. The head was entitled *Metamorphosis*.

Absolutely no knowledge of American Indian iconography was required to decode the image, any more than knowledge of African or Oceanic art would have been necessary to comprehend work by Picasso, Derain, Klee, Gauguin, Vlaminick, Brancusi or many others, in which aboriginal or tribal motifs were exploited. It is true, however, that the anthropologist, archeologist or art historian familiar with Southwest Indian artifacts would recognize a cornucopia of symbolic material. The basic form of the face is derived from the masks of the venerated spirits known as kachinas; kachina masks are worn during sacred and secret ceremonies conducted by the Hopi Indians of Arizona, and by several groups of Pueblo Indians in New Mexico, and are available in vastly vulgarized facsimiles at every trading post in the Southwest, where, as secular "kachina

Metamorphosis, 1981

9

dolls," they are sold in a variety of costumes to tourists. The upper right quadrant of *Metamorphosis* is reminiscent of the Hopi Sun Kachina; the saw-toothed structures at the lower right and the geometric designs throughout are adapted from prehistoric pottery; the elongated blue-green rectangles defining the chin are evocative of *heishi*, the strings of tubular turquoise and shell beads so popular in Indian jewelry outlets in Southwest shopping malls; the coiffure, black and youthful on the left, grey and aged on the right, is a combination of Hopi, Pueblo and Navajo hairstyles; and the disturbing (and disturbed) bull's eye and fanged mouth were adapted from traditional representations of Hehewuti, the Warrior Mother Kachina of the Hopi, who, legend has it, was called upon to defend her village from its enemies, and who went forth to do so half-dressed, her hair done up in a whorl on one side and hanging loose on the other.

The Warrior Mother, the Sun Kachina, pre-Columbian design elements, a sophisticated technique in which layer after layer of acrylic paint is applied laboriously to the surface, sometimes with an atomizer, occasionally with a brush, frequently with an airbrush, often with a pen, less often with a mundane household sponge: *Metamorphosis* could stand as a definitive example of Hardin's art in the early eighties, an art of anger and elegance, of aggressive precision and passionate passivity (the latter a peculiarly Indian trait, paradoxical to the Western mind), an art that seamlessly merged the archeological and the tribal with the contemporary and the personal, an art that sought invariably to return to ancient realms by modern means. "You have noticed that everything an Indian does is in a circle," the Lakota Sioux wiseman Black Elk said, "and that is because the Power of the World always works in circles, and everything tries to be round."

When asked what *Metamorphosis* was, Helen Hardin said, "It's a self-portrait."

From One Soul Two Spirits Come Forth, 1978

TWO

I Have To Try Harder

Hardin's first one-woman show was held at Coronado Monument, a few miles north of Albuquerque, the state's largest city and Hardin's birthplace, when she was nineteen. The year was 1962. Fritz Scholder and R.C. Gorman, whom Hardin would later join in altering irrevocably Anglo attitudes toward Southwest Indian art—attitudes that dismissed modern Indian efforts on the one hand as curios and exalted them on the other as the "pure" aesthetic expressions of a noble, if benighted, people—had yet to attract serious attention. Both men, older than Hardin, had exhibited on a regional basis but she had not heard of them. In 1962, Hardin had heard of very little in the art world and had been exposed to very little art beyond the paintings of her mother, Pablita Velarde, and the paintings of her mother's contemporaries, most of whom continued to work in the so-called "traditional" style developed and formalized thirty years earlier at The Studio, an experiment in programmed art instruction carried out at the Santa Fe Indian School.

Hardin had entered the University of New Mexico and had already spent one summer at a special school conducted by the University of Arizona for potential Indian artists (the school eventually evolved into the Institute of American Indian Art in Santa Fe), but the dark-haired, attractive woman fresh from Catholic high school was at least as interested in dating football players as she was in making any kind of mark in art. "Someone told me when I was in my early twenties that my work reminded them of Kandinsky," she laughed years later, "but I didn't know if that was a compliment: I'd never heard of him. I never got that far in art history. If we did study Kandinsky, I must have been out drinking beer or something." (She was out drinking beer a lot. Friends from those days remember her as ready to try almost anything...twice. "Helen and I shoplifted steaks," one of her college chums said. Hardin had no recollection of the incident, but after imperiously dismissing the possibility, added, "Well, maybe it's possible, after all. But why steaks?")

Messengers of Winter, 1980

13

Coronado Monument is a misnomer; the site is an Indian ruin, a pueblo of 1,200 rooms and six kivas (sacred ceremonial chambers) believed to have been inhabited by the descendants of the prehistoric Anasazi (thought to be the ancestors of the modern-day Hopi and northern Pueblo tribes) from A.D. 1300 to about 1600. The native designation for the village is Kuaua, but the Spanish explorer Francisco Vasquez de Coronado was honored because archeologist Adolf Bandelier (he, too, had an Indian ruin named after him) felt the chroniclers of Coronado's expedition may have referred to the pueblo in one of their dispatches. It is also possible that another Spaniard, Gaspar Perez de Villagra, happened upon the village in 1598 when he wrote: "On the walls of the rooms where we were quartered were many paintings of the demons they worship as gods. Fierce and terrible were their features. It was easy to understand the meaning of these, for the god of water was near the water, the god of the mountains was near the mountains and in like manner all those deities they adore, their gods of the hunt, crops and other things they have."

It is possible because Kuaua, rediscovered in February of 1935 by Edgar L. Hewett and archeologists from the University of New Mexico, the School of American Research and the Museum of New Mexico, contained some of the most significant pre-Columbian images on the continent. (The *fresco secco* polychrome murals, seventeen layers of them, were removed to the Museum of New Mexico; at Kuaua, reproductions of the murals as they appeared at the time of discovery were painted by the Indian artist Ma-Pe-Wi.) Given literal but nonetheless conflicting interpretations by professionals, and poetic but similarly conflicting interpretations by contemporary Indians, the images—birds, animals, plants, stars and masked figures—had long figured in the art of Hardin's mother and had been reproduced by many other contemporary Indian painters. "Though more and finer murals were recovered at other sites later," Maxwell Museum of Anthropology Director J.J. Brody wrote in his doctoral dissertation, published under the title *Indian Painters & White Patrons*, "none created the interest and enthusiasm that the Kuaua murals did."

Bears in the Rainbow House, 1978

Hardin, who had not yet resolved to become an artist but who had been fascinated by picture-making from the time she was a small child, was asked to consider exhibiting her work at Coronado by a group of Plains Indian friends, who had in turn been hired to dance at the public reopening of the monument. Hardin was Tewa, a term identifying a linguistic subdivision of Tanoan stock found in five villages (Tesuque, Nambé, San Ildefonso, Santa Clara, San Juan) of the Rio Grande Valley near Santa Fe, and she was a direct descendant on her mother's side of the Anasazi, the pre-Columbian civilization that spread extensively through the Southwest and left behind the cliff dwellings of Mesa Verde in Colorado, the rock and cave paintings of Arizona's Kayenta region, and the irrigation and road systems of Chaco Canyon in New Mexico. (Her father, Herbert Hardin, was of mixed European extraction.) She had not embarked on a study of her heritage—that would come later—but she had already absorbed through her mother and through her sojourns at her mother's home, Santa Clara Pueblo, a good deal of the imagery that would later appear in altered form in her art.

If she had not committed herself to a career in art—she was in fact negative about the prospect because it would mean competing with her mother, who had achieved the pinnacle of a certain kind of American success by being invited to the White House—the idea of exhibiting at Kuaua was nevertheless irresistible; it was as if a young Greek architect had been asked to display his renderings on the walls of the Parthenon. Her affirmative decision pleased her, it pleased her friends, it pleased the director of the monument, and it pleased her purchasers, but it pleased almost no one else of importance in her life. "My mom was so upset with me," she recalled, "she locked all my Indian clothes up in a trunk and said, 'You can borrow clothes from your friends.'" The extremity of Pablita Velarde's action was partly but not entirely attributable to her drinking; at least as crucial was a chronic battle between mother and daughter that had begun years earlier, a battle that would continue far into Hardin's adult life, a battle characterized by intense competitiveness in the professional arena and distinctly cool relations in the personal. Nor was Hardin likely to receive approval from the elders at Santa Clara Pueblo, as individualistic artistic expression was anathema to the traditional Indian mentality. And not even the most cherished Anglo friends of her youth, Fred and Margarete Chase, owners of Enchanted Mesa, the Native American artifact outlet in Albuquerque, New Mexico, where the art of Velarde had been marketed for years and where the art of Hardin would be sold into the eighties, were pleased. "I didn't get any good strokes at home and I didn't get any good strokes from Fred and Margarete, because they'd always wanted to do my first show; when they wrote about me in their brochures, they always said my first show with them, two years later, was the first to be 'formally presented.'"

That she exhibited, regardless of the consequences, is an indication of how deeply she had accepted values in opposition to Indian culture. "I can see now that I had decided, way back then, to be Anglo socially and Indian in my art. That has never changed." The non-Indian ethics were inculcated not only by her father, as was to be expected, but also, oddly enough, by her mother, whom the elders at Santa Clara had all but ostracized when Velarde undertook to support herself and, in due course, her son Herby and her daughter Helen, by making signed pictures. At nineteen, Hardin was indubitably an Indian; she signed her pictures with her Indian name and its symbol, a spruce tree (under the tree she later added the initials H.H.). She was proficient in Tewa, and although a practicing Roman Catholic, her art was and would remain exclusively non-Christian; however, her refusal to follow her mother's wish that she steer clear of art, her intransigence once she made a decision she felt to be right for her, her open rebelliousness and a style of teenage life dubbed "naughty and nutty" by a high school friend, were not Pueblo traits. To put it mildly. (Publicly, Velarde said she wanted "my Helen" to follow in her footsteps as an artist; privately, she told Hardin her future might be found in business and as late as 1984 was pleased that her daughter was at last putting to use the business training she had encouraged her to obtain in promoting her paintings.) "My Plains Indian friends knew some people out at Cochiti Pueblo, so they borrowed some clothes for me and loaned me some jewelry," Hardin said, by way of concluding the Coronado adventure. "I went to the opening. We pulled it off. It was something I did on my own and it made me feel good."

There was no evidence in the technically talented but in all other respects routine kitsch of the exhibit—"cute little Indian paintings," as Hardin herself dismissed them—that the artist was undergoing difficulties of any description, cultural or psychological, and there was certainly nothing to suggest a fractious future. From the beginning, Hardin separated her art from the turmoil of her life, which is not to imply that her art failed to draw from the events, pleasurable and otherwise, of her life. Far from it: one of her stated aims was to personalize the impersonal inventory of ancient Indian iconography, and at the same time to de-tribalize and de-mystify it, to render its meanings accessible to the non-Indian viewer and to present the same material to the Indian viewer in a new context, transformed by the artist's talent and personality. What she separated from the considerable turmoil of her life—a life that might have given the most outlandish of pulp novelists pangs of imaginative inadequacy—was the act of art-making itself, the process of creation, which became for Hardin what art had been for the Indians of antiquity and what sandpainting remains for the modern Navajo medicineman, an all-consuming attempt, through the placement of line and the choice of color, to restore the harmony of natural forces. She used art as an escape, at a time when there was much from which to escape; she used it as a refuge, at a time when she was a refugee from her own life; and most of all she used it as an act of faith in the future, at a time when she had little reason to believe a different kind of tomorrow would ever come. She painted with an obsessiveness and a perfectionism that transcended economic imperatives. There was a period in her career, in the early seventies, when she painted with an attention to minutiae that transcended *aesthetic* imperatives, a period when her paintings were so full of meticulously executed detail it was impossible for the viewer to appreciate (or even, in some cases, to see) the total complexity of her craftsmanship. There were layers of white on white, and black on black, that were visible only in the brightest sun or under the scrutiny of a magnifying glass. What appears on cursory inspection to be a neutral backdrop for the central figures in *Carriers of the Father Universe* (1974) is actually a complicated white-on-white design, and the eye-fatiguing intricacy of *Recurrence of Spiritual Elements* (1973) speaks for itself. "I don't know any good artists who are not compulsive," Hardin's California dealer, Sue Di Maio, remarked, "and Helen was always compulsive. As compulsive as any, more compulsive than most."

She painted not simply to sell, though her works sold as rapidly as she could paint them, and she painted not merely to become famous, though fame on a regional basis came to her early, and she painted not for simple ego gratification, though her paintings provided more satisfaction than anything else in her life, and she painted not only to express herself in the hallowed individualistic tradition of Western art, though her paintings were more complete representations of the self than anything else she said or did—she painted because she could not *not* paint. "When I was a little girl," she told the crew of a Public Broadcasting System documentary aired in 1976, "I always had this image of artists as terribly lonely people, and probably they can be, if that's the life they create for themselves. I had convinced myself that in order to maintain my career I would have to spend my life alone." She did not remain alone—she married contentedly and reared a daughter happily—but until 1983, when her fight against cancer consumed so much of the time she had once devoted to painting, art was the epicenter of her existence. She understood perfectly what De Kooning was talking about when he declared that the task of modern art was to *"become* life."

Without her obsessiveness, her compulsiveness, her dedication— the term depends on the orientation of the observer—it is unlikely she would have had the strength to persevere in the surreal world of Southwestern art, a world where artistically worthless cowboy landscapes are valued by the inch and are sold into the hundreds of thousands at auctions celebrated in stockyards, where excruciatingly talentless oils of Indians in robes made of tinfoil and gold leaf are hailed as innovative, and where high-pressure techniques that would embarrass a used car salesman are routine. (Long before Hardin's illness was common knowledge, one of her minor dealers took patrons aside, poked his cigar in their faces, and hissed. "Better buy now, she's sick, ya know, Big C. Prices can't do nothing but go up.") But the obstacles facing her had always been formidable. "What's it called?" she asked in the summer of 1982, while entertaining visitors in the living room of the unprepossessing Albuquerque condominium she shared with her husband and daughter, "the car rental agency? Avis? That's it. They try harder. That's me. I try harder. A lot of people consider me the number-one woman Indian artist. I'm categorized as an Indian and then I'm categorized as a woman. So I have to try harder."

Scholder, a one-quarter Mission Indian who studied in California, and Gorman, a Navajo, paved the way for Hardin by authenticating in the minds of the less ethnocentric art critics of the late sixties the "vitality" of Indian art. Questions as to what might in fact constitute Indian art (was it distinct from, or subsumed by, Art?) were vigorously debated by popular and academic commentators. The pictorial, predictable scenes that had been the hallmark of The Studio style—the "cute little Indian pictures" that earned Hardin's contempt—had controlled Southwestern Indian art for three decades. With the exception of rare individuals such as the Sioux painter Oscar Howe or the Pueblo artist Joe H. Herrera, the stagnation was close to complete. Scholder and Gorman declared open war against The Studio. The latter took as his models the Mexican muralists Orozco, Siqueiros and Rivera, and announced, "There is no such thing as a contemporary Indian painting." (Hardin was at this moment blithely signing the back of each piece, "A Contemporary Indian Painting by Helen Hardin.")

In his manifestos, Gorman looked forward to a future of acceptance and integration—he fell into the melting pot. "I think that Indian painting shall have made a contribution to American culture on the day when I can walk into a bookstore and pick up a book titled *American Painters* and find the Indians are included. So much for Audubon and Andy Warhol!" But the most likely candidate for inclusion in any such book was not Gorman, it was Scholder, who vowed in 1964 (the year of Hardin's first "formal" solo show at Enchanted Mesa) that he would never paint another Indian. "The non-Indian," he declared, "had painted the subject as a noble savage and the Indian painter had been caught in a tourist-pleasing cliché." He changed his mind when he resolved to invent "a new idiom in Indian painting," an idiom summarized by an aphorism: "I have painted the Indian real, not red."

At its peak, the work of both men justified the many shamelessly laudatory regional reviews that came their way. The paintings also earned, through their unimpeachable integrity and "shocking" innovation, even more heartening and worthy accolades: scathing critiques and running-scared dismissals from the Southwestern art establishment. Gorman's Navajo rug studies were minor masterpieces. His fusion of traditional Navajo decorative motifs with a celebration of texture and color for their own sake, an approach he borrowed from the abstract expressionists, resulted in an art at once identifiably Indian and incontrovertibly contemporary. Similarly, Scholder's unflatteringly smeary, emotional portraits of Indians hit the viewer accustomed to the idealized Kodachrome kitsch of commercialized Indian art with the force of a fist in the face; the agonized, meaty heads could have illustrated consummately, "Drunken Indians," Calvin Trillin's 1973 report for *The New Yorker* on Gallup, New Mexico, a trading-post town catering to Navajo consumers. But as the seventies wore on, Gorman succumbed to the speed of lithography, and, entranced by the popularity of his nudes—women of fleshy Rubenesque plenitude—verged on becoming the Vargas of Indian art. His excesses, including an illustrated cookbook, *Nudes and Foods,* and his willingness to exploit his personal iconography in any medium (there were Gorman nudes engraved as single-line drawings on huge ceramic vases; Gorman nudes woven into nubby carpets; Gorman nudes comporting themselves on greeting cards) earned him another sobriquet, the Reservation Dali. In the eighties,

Gorman bought a gallery in the Old Town section of Albuquerque, a magnificent outlet devoted solely, with a single exception, to the work of R.C. Gorman. The exception: a lithograph, *Who is R.C. Gorman?*, by the young Navajo artist Ed Singer. That the lithograph might be satirical may not have occurred to the house's artist-in-perpetual-residence.

More than any other Native artist, Scholder was an inspiration to Hardin, but not because she responded to his art *qua* art. By refusing to follow the accepted canons of "good taste" for Indians, Scholder was a true revolutionary, Hardin believed. "He showed Indians what they could do if they wanted to, he showed them the way." She was in his debt, and she knew it. Scholder rebuffed commercialization as totally as Gorman embraced it; the former specialized in quality, the latter in quantity. Scholder preferred galleries that handled no other Indian artist. He rejected, out-of-hand, double exhibitions with jewelers, a common practice of Southwestern dealers. In terms of Native art, his prices were astronomical: $30,000 for major paintings. They sold. So many of them sold, he posed for pictures in front of a Rolls. His. He was intent on being accepted as an artist who happened to be Indian, and he had his own model of what being an artist meant: the British painter Francis Bacon. Scholder first saw examples of Bacon's refined Expressionism at the Tate Gallery during a 1969 trip to London. The shock of the new stuck. While his landscapes, electrically colored vistas influenced by Georgia O'Keeffe, were untouched (they in turn influenced Scholder's skillful variants, John Nieto and Dan Namingha), the line that could be drawn in his figure paintings, pre- and post-Bacon, was less a line than a canyon. The strongest work in the spirit of Bacon did effect a powerful pairing of Southwestern satire and Angst-on-the-Thames—in the best work, the color was a volcanic spew of ferocious Fauvism, and the caricatures that passed as portraiture were redolent of the dust and beer and body odor of reservation skid-row bars. In the mediocre work, however, the feeling that the viewer was witnessing a gifted reproduction of what Francis Bacon might have made of a trip to New Mexico could not be dispelled. (There is little

Hohokam Shadows, 1983

doubt that if a wholly white painter had dared offer an image corresponding, say, to Scholder's *Screaming Indian* of 1970, he would instantly have been castigated as a racist.)

Scholder continued to evolve far from the Indian iconography that made him famous: had Hardin lived to see his development, she would no doubt have applauded it. Her emotional reactions to Gorman and Scholder were, in any event, complex. Hardin could not draw free-hand easily or well, and Gorman was a master of single-line compositions. Hardin could not paint spontaneously easily or at all, and Scholder was a master of the knocked-off but nonetheless inspired canvas. (Hardin did have a sense of humor regarding the technically armored nature of her work, however: a close friend, Susan Brooke, revealed to Kristina Ryder [author of an unpublished master's thesis on Hardin] that the artist once said her paintings were so indestructible they could probably withstand the Timex tire test and promptly drove over one of them to prove it. The painting emerged with its surface intact.)

On the subject of Scholder, Hardin was privately vitriolic for years. (Her mother was even more obsessed: she was certain Scholder was in cahoots with evil spirits and would spit on the ground to protect herself at his approach.) In Hardin's younger years, Scholder represented everything she hated about the macho mystique of the Indian male (despite the fact that she did not accept him as an Indian): "If you said 'Fritz Scholder,' I'd throw up on the floor and roll in it, and have a temper tantrum and go out and get drunk for three days. That's how much I hated it," she told Ryder in 1984. In the gossipy lore of Southwestern art, Hardin-Scholder tiffs (they served on several juries together) were traded with delight. Hardin was said to have told Scholder, in response to his request for an explanation of the meaning of one of her titles, "If you were Indian, you'd know," and she was also reputed to have informed him that if he were punched in the nose, "You would lose all your Indian blood in five minutes." (Coming from a woman who was half-white, the insult may have lacked some of its oomph.) After Hardin's death, Scholder professed gallantly to remember little of the bickering. "But I think,"

Guardians of the Sun, 1984

he added, "that Helen may have thought, as so many did, thanks to the publicity, that I was posing as an 'Indian artist,' which I never did." He was correct: as far back as 1975, he declared, "To tell the truth, I don't know what Indian art is," and in 1980, he announced that his Indian series was concluded and he would henceforth paint no more Indian images. He was as good as his word: his single departure was *Medicine Woman* (1981), executed as a favor to a writer friend who wanted an Indian-themed image for a book jacket.

But Scholder understood Hardin's antipathy—and her jealousy. "T.C. Cannon, my best Indian student (he died in a car accident in 1978) used to call me in the middle of the night to talk about the pain. Indians brainwash their children with an incredible hatred of the white man and then expect them to get along in a white man's world. I came in and painted all this conflict and pain, almost as a journalist. But for me, the Indian series was a series, not a way of life. For Indians, that was difficult to accept. And of course my success with the series made it doubly difficult. Helen, to top it all off, had all those problems with her mother. And she was trying to live in two worlds at once. Tough; but a tough lady."

On a purely professional level, watching these two careers was sobering for Hardin. She could not conceive of undertaking the promotion necessary to become an R.C. Gorman, nor could she imagine turning her highly spiritual images into carpets and cookbooks. She did not care to decorate vases. And while she admired and emulated Scholder's high seriousness, his art was antipodal to hers. His initial thrust was political and psychological and satirical, not spiritual and metaphysical and mythological; he was indifferent to the ancient patterns she was absorbed by; his style was superficially loose, improvisatory and painterly—European, by way of action painting—while hers was tight, precise and geometric—pre-Columbian, by way of mechanical drawing. His greatest influences were individualistic European artists; hers were the anonymous craftsmen of the Mimbres and Mogollon and Hohokam cultures of a thousand years ago. Hardin agreed with Scholder and Gorman that if by traditional Indian art one meant The Studio's aesthetic heirs, traditional Indian art was bankrupt. To her, the authentic aboriginal tradition was to be found in the primal imagery of the pictograph and the petroglyph, in the geometry of the Navajo blanket and the whimsy of the Zia bird, in the monumentality of the Hopi kachina and the delicate designs of the Tewa *tablita* (a headdress worn during religious ceremonies). She rejected picture-postcard views of happy Indians herding immaculate sheep but she also felt a strong aversion to the idea of eschewing Indian imagery altogether. She had a heritage; she wanted to express it. Added to her condundrum was an additional difficulty experienced by neither Gorman nor Scholder, an acute personal ambivalence that would cause her great pain the rest of her life.

When Hardin claimed, as she did in interview after interview, that she was not a traditional painter and that she thought The Studio was a dead issue, a spent force, she was not speaking in the abstract about a movement she found temperamentally inhospitable, as a minimalist might clinically dismiss an impressionist. She was talking about and dismissing a movement that had quite literally reared her; she was talking about her own early work, of course, but she was also talking about her mother's lifework. The Velarde sisters, Pablita and Rosita, were the only women in attendance on a full-time basis at The Studio in 1932, the year it was founded by Dorothy Dunn, and Pablita was to become its most honored female graduate — "the greatest woman artist of the Southwest" (Clara Lee Tanner, *Southwest Indian Art,* second edition, 1973). In Hardin's effort to assert her own aesthetic identity and artistic independence, it was a characterization she would set out methodically to overthrow.

THREE
Someday It Will All Be A Dream

Hardin's mother, the third child of Santa Clara farmer and trapper Herman Velarde and his wife Marianita, was born on September 18, 1918, but was not named until four days later in a ceremony conducted by the baby's maternal grandmother, the medicinewoman Qualupita. At Santa Clara, an impoverished village accustomed to staggeringly high infant mortality rates, no child was named immediately—it was thought to require at least four days for the human spirit to enter the infant's body. When the prescribed waiting period had elapsed, the child was called Tse Tsan, or Golden Dawn in English. (Twenty-five years later, the aged Qualupita would choose for Helen Hardin a Tewa name meaning Blue Corn Tassels, but Herman Velarde rejected it in favor of Tsa-Sah-Wee-Eh, Little Standing Spruce, his wife Marianita's Indian name.) Neither Tse Tsan nor Golden Dawn would follow their owner into renown; for that, there would be Velarde—Spanish surnames were imposed on the people of the pueblos when, in 1692, Don Diego de Vargas quashed the Pueblo Rebellion of 1680, ending forever the autonomy of the indigenous population—and Pablita, the Spanish version of Pauline, the female version of Paul, the Roman Catholic saint. Until Tse Tsan and her two older sisters, Standing Cloud and Flower (or Legoria and Rosita, respectively, in Spanish), were sent to boarding school in Santa Fe, the state capitol thirty miles to the south, she did not know that she had an alternative name.

"My mother," Hardin remarked, "grew up angry." With reason. When six-year-old Tse Tsan arrived at St. Catherine's Indian School, an institution operated by a missionary order, the Sisters of the Blessed Sacrament, she spoke not a word of English; the nuns spoke not a word of Tewa. It would take several days for the frightened baby of the trio to conceptualize fully the identity of the "Pablita" whom the nuns insisted on addressing, and it would take several weeks for the linguistic gibberish surrounding her to sort itself out. The three girls had already suffered acute feelings of abandon-

Pablita Velarde's parents on their wedding day; taken at Santa Clara Pueblo, New Mexico, circa 1910. (Courtesy Pablita Velarde)

29

ment—their mother had died three years earlier, of a disease thought variously to be tuberculosis or influenza—and it now seemed to them that their desertion by their parents was complete. Their father visited only twice, and then only briefly, the first year they were in Santa Fe and at no point suggested they return to the pueblo on their fall and spring vacations. Joined in due course by a still younger sister, Jane (Little Turquoise Ray), the girls did go home during the summer, but as Pablita Velarde grew, her estrangement from her family also grew. Each ensuing event compounded the alienation and the anger. Her father married again; his wife, Clara Naranjo, died two years later while giving birth to a son—the boy lived a mere three months. By the time Pablita had completed elementary school and had entered the United States Indian School in Santa Fe as an eighth grader in the company of Rosita (the staff allowed the precocious Pablita to skip the seventh grade), her father was once again wed. This wife, Rose, who was in her late teens and was therefore not much older than Legoria, earned the everlasting enmity of Herman Velarde's girls. ("My grandfather and his daughters did make peace, but never with that last wife," Hardin said. "She lasted the longest. She lasted forever: she outlived my grandfather. She was an alcoholic and died of cirrhosis.") When Legoria dropped out of school at fifteen to marry a nineteen-year-old Santa Clara man, Pasqual, it was to Legoria's home that Pablita, Rosita and Jane came on vacations, not to the house inhabited by her father and his new family.

Velarde enrolled in the United States Indian School, operated by the Bureau of Indian Affairs, in September of 1932. On the ninth day of the same month, an art teacher from Chicago opened under the auspices of the school a painting studio with a definite ideological and aesthetic mission. Dorothy Dunn was not out to encourage her forty students to become artists or craftsmen adept in mainstream expression, though she was quick to realize there was an "element" in her classes that expected the school "to provide quick training in the accomplishments of the modern non-Indian American, which they thought would enable them to cope with the latter on equal terms." Dunn had a very different concept of the ways in which the former might compete with the latter; in a spirit of accommodation but never of assimilation, she set out to maintain the Indian as separate but equal, and to encourage the exploitation of what *she* defined as Native tradition. "Any production which revealed copy of *unworthy exotic influences* was discouraged, not by forbiddance, but by suggestion of a variety of tribal elements which might make a particular painting more *authentic* or *interesting*," she wrote of her modus operandi (italics supplied).

This was standard-issue liberal paternalism of the thirties. In their 1931 introduction to the catalogue of The Exposition of Indian Tribal Arts, an exhibition that opened in New York in November of that year with advertisements hailing it as the first collection of artifacts to be "selected entirely with consideration of aesthetic value," John Sloan and the Pulitzer Prize-winning novelist Oliver LaFarge began their defense of indigenous art with an astonishing statement: "The American Indian possesses an innate talent in the fine and applied arts. The Indian is a born artist; possessing a capacity for discipline and careful work, and a fine sense of line and rhythm, which seems to be inherent in the Mongoloid peoples." ("White people still think every Indian is talented and creative," Hardin observed. "And they're always sure I make my own jewelry. It's almost a matter of principle when I tell them, 'No, I only do wall art.'") Well-intentioned these white patrons and educators were; well-versed in Indian ethnography there were not. As J.J. Brody argued persuasively and at length in *Indian Painters & White Patrons*, "authenticity" was in the eye of Dorothy Dunn; "authentic" Pueblo paintings existed on the walls of kivas and were ceremonial in nature. Period.

"I met Dorothy Dunn in 1932," Velarde remembered in late 1983 during an interview conducted in the extremely modest Albuquerque home she had occupied since 1947. "She started this studio with a class of mostly boys. I was taking craft lessons and I wasn't all that interested, so I though I'd try drawing and painting. I told Miss Morrow, who was my craft teacher, that I was going to enroll over there at Dorothy Dunn's art class and she got mad at me. I wasn't doing so good anyway—she ought to have been glad to get rid of me. I made my older sister Rosita come with me so I wouldn't be the only girl in there. The boys at class used to be so mean about it, and would say, 'Go get a job in the kitchen,' stuff like that. They were real chauvinist types. Rosita got married after a few months but I stayed on."

Velarde had no notion of what she was getting into. The "chauvinist types" among the males in her class were not simply or even anti-female, they were merely giving vent to traditional tribal attitudes; women made pots in the pueblo, but they never decorated kiva walls; painting was an exclusively male preserve. That the boys did not become more incensed at Velarde than they did is an indication of how disorienting the school was for them as well. Dunn noticed "it had not occurred to most students to think of their native art as *art*. Indian art was something accepted without thinking about it, as part of everyday life…" and it is likely that few of the boys equated what they were producing for the enthusiastic white woman with the ritualized images on the kiva walls.

If Dunn's declarations regarding what she saw as intrinsic Indian abilities had a tradition, so too did her encouragement of Indian "tradition" itself. As early as the nineteenth century, traders anxious to augment their earnings, and in some cases to lessen the horrifying poverty of the Indians with whom they traded, sponsored "craft revivals"—jewelry and rugs for the Navajo, pottery and jewelry in the pueblos. But the true beginning of modern Indian art, for good and ill, may date from the glancing relationship of anthropologist Jesse W. Fewkes and the Indian potter Nampeyo, a woman from the Tewa village of Hano on the Hopi Reservation. Nampeyo was introduced in the summer of 1895 to pottery unearthed by Fewkes and his Native assistants at Sikyatki, an ancestral Hopi home in ruins, and she found in the graceful geometry of its design and in the dusty mustards and earthy terra-cottas of its polychrome coloration an inspiration that led to a revival of Hopi pottery. (Years later, Hardin's homage to her aesthetic ancestor would take the form of the painting *Hopi Illusion,* 1980, patterned after one of Nampeyo's pots; the bright blues and glossy blacks deliberately departed from Nampeyo's muted polychrome scheme but when Hardin redesigned the image

Hopi Illusion,
four-color etching, 1980

as a four-color etching, she restored the warm earthen tones. The result was simultaneously delicate, archaic and yet oddly sophisticated, the work of a pre-Columbian Paul Klee.)

Thanks to her ancestors, Nampeyo's personal fortunes were secure. With the exception of Maria Martinez, "the potter of San Ildefonso," whose revival of a black-on-black decorative technique occasioned an unprecedented and to this day unmatched publicity uproar, Nampeyo became the most respected Indian artist of her time and was asked to perform her craft publicly in Chicago (at the behest of the Santa Fe Railway) and at the Grand Canyon (for the Fred Harvey Company). Meanwhile, anthropologists Edgar L. Hewett and Kenneth Chapman followed Fewkes's lead, Hewett at San Ildefonso with Maria Martinez and her husband Julian, and Chapman at Santo Domingo with the Aguilar sisters. (A revival at Santa Clara of incised black-on-black pottery commenced much later in the thirties; Legoria was instrumental in the renaissance.)

The indefatigable Fewkes did not confine his blandishments to pottery. Some five years after he introduced Nampeyo to her heritage, he hired four Hopi men to draw two hundred pictures of kachinas, sacred spirits common to Hopi and Pueblo Indians. The drawings bore some stylistic resemblance to what little was known of contemporary ceremonial art and to prehistoric murals, but their creation at the behest of a white man for documentary rather than ritual purposes was an innovation. Fewkes included the pictures in *Codex Hopiensis,* and the artifacts in this Native American bestiary—the magisterial Sun Kachina, the half-human and half-earthen mudhead spirits, the zebra-striped koshare clown—do, as Dunn wrote, "show great vitality. Potential action is evident even in the perfectly balanced, motionless representations. Animation is largely effected by color vibration and bold patterning."

There were other sporadic outbursts of artistic activity—Api-Begay, a Navajo, drew on cardboard boxes found by Chapman at a trading post near Pueblo Bonita in Chaco Canyon in 1901; four drawings of kachinas by Hopi children at the Sherman Institute in Riverside, California, were forwarded to the Smithsonian in 1908 with a note from the teacher praising them as exceptional "for untutored savages"—but the first significant Indian painters were Alfredo Montoya and Crescenio Martinez, both of San Ildefonso. About the former almost nothing is known except that he apparently painted to bring extra money to his village; the latter, in contrast, worked for Hewett during excavations of ruins on the Parajito Plateau and informed the white scientist that he could paint pictures similar to those being found at the site. In the summer of 1917, Martinez brought Hewett several examples. Hewett requested more, and Martinez dutifully painted them. "In January 1918," Hewett wrote, "he gave me a careful explanation of all the cardinal figures and costumes as he understood them and I commissioned him to paint a complete series of designs. The first twelve he finished and delivered late in winter. These he signed. The last ten were finished in the spring. He lacked only one (the second eagle) of finishing the commission. He completed the first eagle just a few days before his death. It was his last work."

On June 20, 1918, three months before Velarde's birth, Martinez fell victim to influenza. Inspired by his example, other San Ildefonso Indians devoted their energies to art, but one of them, Quah Ah (whose Spanish name was Tonita Peña and who became the first Indian woman easel artist on record), actually preceded Martinez as a painter. Dunn reports that Peña, a San Ildefonso native who moved to nearby Cochiti pueblo as a child, had been painting from the age of six but did not make her work known to "the San Ildefonso school" until the advent of Martinez—she and Alfredo Montoya had been classmates, and both children had been encouraged to draw and paint by Esther B. Hoyt, an elementary school teacher at San Ildefonso. Evaluating her work in later years, Dunn wrote, "Quah Ah's art is an art of radiance and tranquility. It is possessed of delicacy and grace, and much music. It is unequalled at conveying the dignity, the serenity, the great earnestness and wholehearted sincerity of the Pueblo ceremonial and the Pueblo people. Quah Ah's work is not ever spectacular or striking, but it is completely unpretentious and authentic. She might be called a conservative painter for she has set her own standards in keeping with tradition and has adhered to them through the years so consistently that, even beyond her death, she has never been superceded as the dean of Indian women painters."

Peña's "authenticity" is a moot point, but she was certainly not traditional or conservative. No Pueblo woman who painted could be: if her art did not bespeak changing times, its very existence did. When Velarde met Peña, she was attracted to her immediately. Though too old to be a student, Peña was employed by the government on a mural project and lived in the Indian School dormitory. "She spoke Tewa, like I did," Velarde said, her affection still palpable in 1983. "I used to visit her in her room. She would talk to me like a mother to a daughter and give me all this advice. 'Who cares what the men think?' she would say." As the setting sun struck Velarde's strong, flat features—she was a physical paradox, statuesque in strength and petite in stature, like the late blues singer Alberta Hunter—she giggled softly, a signal that a statement of assertion or aggression, unseemly by Pueblo standards, had emerged and required diffident punctuation. "I thought, she doesn't care what they think, so why should I care? (Giggle) I think she kind of planted a seed. She was the first, what do they call women nowadays?, she was the first liberated woman. 'Who cares what the men think, as long as you are happy?' (Giggle) I admired her very much."

Between the individualism of Peña and the collectivism of Pueblo life, where the emphasis was always and forever on the harmony of the community—and on the harmony of the community within the larger harmony of nature—there was a chasm of acculturation and de-tribalization. Velarde was already alienated from her family; to complete the process, she needed only to become alienated from her people, and that she accomplished in her choice of vocation. When she was barely out of the eighth grade, a painting was sent to the Century of Progress exhibit in Chicago; the painting was a success, she was a success and she was fussed over continually at The Studio. Santa Fe was positive and reinforcing and even loving. Santa Clara was none of those things. She signed up for another year at The Studio. "The second year there were a few more girls that got brave enough and joined," she remembered, "so it was better. That first year, I took a lot of teasing from the boys, and insults as well. I didn't care. (Giggle) I just thought, I'm going to listen to Tonita and not to you. (Giggle) I was there to learn and I put my mind to it. I knew I wasn't a great painter yet."

"It is heresy among primal peoples such as Indians for someone to depart from the communal mentality," Jamake Highwater wrote in his essay-length history of modern Indian art, *The Sweet Grass Lives On.* "It is also heresy among some Indians for a Native American to attain sophistication. One thing conservative Indians and non-Indians seem to agree about is that 'good' Indians are supposed to remain pure, which means static. So intense is this attitude toward Indian purity that a sophisticated and articulate Indian is not considered to be *really* Indian. In fact, the Indian regard for conformity is so intense that psychologists working with urbanized Native people have often pointed up the fact that their individuated patients suffer the same sort of intense guilt *toward their tribes* that rebellious whites suffer in relationship *to their parents.*"

The rift in the relationship with Herman Velarde would be repaired and Pablita would be claimed as an asset by the elders of Santa Clara when it suited their purposes, but she would never be reintegrated. In 1966, she attempted to act as a cultural anthropologist by recording the reminiscences of Santa Clarans but was forced to halt the project when she felt "evil spirits"—whether of the dead or living, she did not know—arrayed against her. "My mother always talks about going back to the pueblo to live permanently," Hardin said. "She's afraid. She's afraid she'll be ostracized again."

Velarde was equally frank, and more than a little wistful. "I have a home at the pueblo," she said. "I only use it as someplace to park when I'm up there. I'm in Albuquerque most of the time. Some of the people at the pueblo are very grateful that I have migrated into the white world and have brought change by encouraging the young ones to get training. I'm always preaching up there, 'Get your education.' In the last few years there's been a lot of painters coming up.

Somewhere along the line I imagine they decided, 'If that old lady can do it, I can too.' I don't take credit for anything that happens at the pueblo, though, because my association[s] with my own people [are] far and few. The pueblo will survive but it will have a different atmosphere. Everybody's getting very modern. They like all the conveniences. They like everything the easy way. You can't blame them. When I was growing up, it was all back-breaking work. Maybe that's why I turned to art. It wasn't so back-breaking. I used to see those ladies working from sunup to sundown, getting old fast. I felt sorry for them but I didn't want to be like them. I stayed here because I didn't want the children to grow up as I had. I got used to it, all this rat race I got myself into. I grinned and bore it and I stayed here."

Velarde graduated from the Indian School in 1936, the first in her family to receive a high school diploma (Rosita had followed Legoria's lead and dropped out to get married). She returned to Santa Clara, found a job as an assistant day-school instructor for two years and was hired to travel as a glorified nanny to the offspring of naturalist author and Boy Scouts of America founder Ernest Thompson Seton (*Wild Animals I Have Known*). When she returned from the trip that had taken her north to New England and south to Arkansas, she received two welcome commissions, the first to contribute to the façade of Maisel's jewelry store in downtown Albuquerque, the second to illustrate at Bandelier National Monument "the daily life of the pueblos." With confidence in her artistry acquired from Dunn, she forged ahead: "Dorothy Dunn's been my one and only teacher. The rest is self-taught. They say a lot now against Dorothy Dunn. I was grateful. She had to start someplace. She was new in the game just like we were." The game was at first ephemeral; in 1940, when National Park Service funding was redirected to the armed forces, Velarde was let go and forced to find work elsewhere. A year later she was ensconced, securely but unhappily, as a switchboard operator at the Bureau of Indian Affairs office in Albuquerque. She had a feeling things would get better.

Pablita Velarde, 1938, during her stay with the family of naturalist Seton. (Courtesy Pablita Velarde)

Her niche as an artist was already well formed—her niche, and her prison. Her techniques would improve but her aims would seldom vary. She excelled at genre scenes and she was adept at reproducing facsimiles of ancient forms. She was not inventive, however, and was not encouraged to be. Her buyers were pleased by her tempera and casein (milk-based paint) studies, and especially by the "earth paintings" she perfected in the fifties, a modernization of the sandpaintings of the Navajo, accomplished by grinding natural pigments to powder, liquifying them in a glue base and applying them to a board with a brush. The procedure was time-consuming—each layer of powder had to dry fully before another could join it—but the results were profitable. Looking back on her career at the age of sixty-five, she was modest. "My most important development is my storytelling paintings. I wasn't all that interested in storytelling until I hit about forty and then it began to dawn on me that no one was telling stories any more. In 1960, I published my book of stories and paintings, *Old Father the Story Teller.*" She pointed to what may be her finest painting, a rhapsodic representation of a storyteller and the mythic migrations of his people. "My dad was a good storyteller and so was my grandfather, and also my grandmother, and I remember this one old uncle, he was real skinny, a bony kind of person, and at evening time, he would gather all the relatives together and tell stories. All the kids would fall asleep before the stories ended, but the adults went on, telling story after story, until they got tired too, and went home. That was their way of entertainment and I thought it was pretty neat. When I painted that painting, I thought of my old uncle."

She sat back, exhausted, in a battered armchair. "It's all gone now. I'm trying to bring it back by going into the schools and telling stories and I'm trying to get their interest revived again to be a listener instead of a watcher, you know—that darned television. My work is…documentary, I guess. I think if I leave enough paintings it will be an education for everybody about very true things that happened in the pueblo. I'm going to leave something that is eventually going to die anyway. Someday it will all be a dream."

This piece, Old Father the Story Teller, *was painted by Pablita Velarde circa 1960 and is typical of her style.*

FOUR

You Have To Be Where You Aren't

When Pablita Velarde's sinecure at Bandelier National Monument fell victim to budget cuts, she was surprisingly unperturbed; although only twenty-three years old, she was accustomed to acting independently—she had already built a house for herself at Santa Clara—and without much fuss, made her way to Albuquerque. There she found her job as a switchboard operator, and there, while fielding calls on the nightshift, she struck up a conversation with an Anglo security guard, Herbert Hardin. Velarde was attracted to Hardin's manner and she approved of his ambition to become a lawyer. He in turn found her to be equally attractive and, for an Indian girl, amazingly loquacious—in his experience, Indian women would smile and they might giggle, but they seldom spoke, and almost never to a white man. On Valentine's Day 1941, Velarde became Mrs. Herbert Hardin.

The next five years were a symphony of separation. Velarde followed Herbert to Bastrop, Texas, but when she became pregnant, returned to Albuquerque to give birth on May 28, 1943, to a daughter she christened Helen. A month later, she was at Santa Clara to participate in the ceremony that bestowed upon the baby the Indian name Tsa-Sah-Wee-Eh. Five months later, the family was reunited in Pennsylvania, where Herbert was stationed; when his posting was switched to California, Velarde returned once more to New Mexico to give birth, this time to a boy, Herby, on August 13, 1944. Then, the war over, Herbert Hardin came home and told his wife he had decided, in the interests of economy, to study criminology instead of law. The Hardins moved to Richmond, California, to allow Herbert to enter the University of California at Berkeley, but Velarde rapidly developed a severe case of asthma in the comparatively muggy coastal air and was advised by her doctor to leave California. On taking Helen and Herby back to the house at Santa Clara, she discovered that her old job as artist-in-residence at Bandelier was open; she accepted the assignment happily. Herbert, meanwhile,

Helen and her father, Herbert Hardin, during one of his army leaves; photograph taken circa 1944.

The Hardin family—Herbert, Pablita, Helen, and Herby—in front of their first house; located in Albuquerque, New Mexico, the house is now surrounded by large trees and bushes.

graduated in June of 1947 and by October had been taken on as a rookie cop at the Albuquerque Police Department. Velarde's art career continued apace—she made an important sale in 1948 to the Philbrook Art Museum in Tulsa, and was beginning to win prizes— and it was therefore with relief that she was able to send her perkily inexhaustible and demanding daughter to Zia Elementary School. Because no provision had been made for a studio in the house she and Herbert bought on Adams Street Northeast near the University of New Mexico, she painted on the kitchen table. The intrusion of her children and their friends was a constant distraction.

Helen Hardin had one indelible memory of her introduction to undiluted Anglo culture at Zia. "When I was a child on the reservation, I had never seen Santa Claus. I had heard him on the radio, but I had never been to a department store where I could have seen him— I had no idea what he looked like. None. All I knew was that he brought presents. In the first grade my teacher passed out some mimeographed sheets with a drawing of Santa with his sack full of toys going down the chimney. She told us, 'Okay, now color these.' I looked around and everyone had picked up a red crayon. So I took out my purple crayon and went to work on his suit. My coloring was impeccable: it always was, it was in the lines, everything went the same direction. Except Santa was purple. Then I colored the sky black. When we got our papers back I had a big red F on mine. She must have thought I was being rebellious deliberately. I thought she didn't like me. She never said anything to me about it and I never asked. It never occurred to her I might not have seen Santa Claus."

The childhood years were otherwise uneventful and contrary to what might have been expected, devoid of racial prejudice. "Being an Indian kind of made me neat to the other girls. It sort of set me apart and made me wonderful. Nobody ever disliked me because I was an Indian, but there were a lot of kids who didn't like me because I was fat. I felt bad about being fat. I never felt bad about being an Indian. I never had any problems, in those days, with religion, either. My mother told me the Pueblo stories, but when some Baptist neighbors invited me and my brother to Sunday School, my mom said yes, and we went for about a year. All we did was cut out paper and sing songs about Jesus. I didn't know who Jesus was. I didn't *really* know until I was about eight, when my mother decided that maybe she should bring us up Catholics because she'd made all these promises when she married my father. She went to see a priest and we started going to catechism on Saturdays. I remember I didn't learn as much about Jesus as I did about the rules of the Catholic Church, and I remember all these terrible things the nuns would tell us, like we'd go to hell if we missed Mass. When I was a kid, being a Catholic and being an Indian had nothing to do with each other. Being an Indian and learning all the stories was one thing and being white and Catholic was something else."

The attitude was formed at home. "Indians ignore one religion," Velarde explained, "and then go into another. They'll ignore the Christian and pay attention to the Indian, then they'll come back to the Christian and ignore the Indian. It's like being in a house with two different rooms. They're different rooms, but they're the same house. I'm one of those with two religions. I turn them off and on. I have painted scenes from the Bible. I have my Christmas cards, but of course my theme was Indian, I created Indian characters instead of people I didn't know anything about way over there in Bethlehem. The only way I could say Merry Christmas was to put up two cliff walls with a Navajo blanket, instead of a stable, and I put a little bonfire on the desert in front of them to keep them warm."

The only way Hardin, a practicing Catholic, could eventually make peace with the Catholic Church was to realize that "everything the nuns told us was bullshit." But her mother's ability to turn religion off and on like a light was lost on her: in Hardin's house, there was room for only one room. "I think my Helen respects the way the Indian people perform in ceremonials and believe, but it doesn't create an inspiration for her, except in her art," Velarde conjectured accurately. Interestingly, Velarde accepted two religions and painted imagery inspired by each, while Hardin accepted one religion and never painted its iconography. "When I was in Catholic high school," she said, "I painted all the Christian subjects I will ever do. I got it out of my system. It was like painting portraits or landscapes: I did it all, but it was boring. Pictures of adobes are still boring to me, unless they're by Georgia O'Keeffe. When I painted Indian subjects, a sense of Indian-ness would be there, a spiritual element I can't explain. The only thing that did bother me, once I began painting seriously, was that one of the commandments was 'Thou shalt have no other gods before me' and I thought, 'Oh my God, what are these kachinas doing in my life?' I didn't give the kachinas any real religious homage, but I felt if I were going to be a real Indian I would have to, so I decided I was not going to be a real Indian, because the Catholic Church had already frightened me to death about God. I decided to continue to be frightened to death about God—and keep my kachinas."

Kachinas provided Hardin with her richest imagery and her most unfailing inspiration; they were a constant in her career, and she could not imagine being without them. The kachina cosmology of the Hopi and Pueblo Indians is not easy for the non-Indian to grasp—the spirits are more than human, less than divine, and while they are venerated, they are not worshipped. Hardin compared kachinas to the saints of the Catholic Church, to Saint Jude, the patron saint of lost causes, for example, or to other saints with other patronages: "There are saints for everything, and it's the same with kachinas. They are a series of spirits responsible for things. They are represented in different ways. Some of them wear clothes, some of them wear none, some of them wear more clothes than others." Kachinas are similar to saints in an additional, if superficial, respect: they come and go. Kachinas are born, evolve and then die, much as Saint Christopher came and went, but without official proclamation and investigation. "They appear and disappear with the ebb and flow of time, like life itself," Frank Waters wrote in *Book of the Hopi,* "and they are as legion as [life's] infinite forms." Tradition has it they enter the earth through the San Francisco Peaks, south of Oraibi near Flagstaff, Arizona, but Waters's Hopi informants told him "they come from much farther away, a long, long way — from neighboring stars, constellations too distant to be visible, from mysterious spirit worlds." Hardin agreed: when asked if it bothered her that uninitiated viewers sometimes interpreted her kachinas as extraterrestrials, she shrugged, "They are; they come from the stars."

For Tewa Indians, the kachinas' primary duties are pragmatic: they are sought as intermediaries responsible for rain, for the growing of corn, for fecundity in both botanical and biological manifestations. They are, as Waters put it, "the inner forms, the spiritual components of the outer physical forms of life, which may be invoked to manifest their benign powers so that man may be enabled to continue his never-ending journey. They are the invisible forces of life — not gods, but rather intermediaries, messengers." Their features are on display only during ceremonials, and only in the form of masks worn by the elders of the village; revealing the exact configurations of those masks outside the pueblo is forbidden. "I was told not to paint kachinas by the elders at home when I started painting," Velarde recalled. "They said, 'You can paint anything you want, a koshare is fine' — koshare is a sort of clown kachina, he's striped and sometimes has a watermelon — 'but anything past a koshare we don't want you to paint.' I did paint koshare, and so did Helen (*Watermelon Break,* 1978), but I have never painted my kachinas. I

borrowed a Hopi kachina once in a while when I wanted to get different, but my own I have never painted. I *couldn't.* Helen has never seen them. I never took her into the kiva when the ceremonies were being performed. I have never taken either child into the kiva. Well, I think once I did, when they were real small, but their memory won't carry them this far."

"I do remember being in the kiva once when I was very small," Hardin laughed. "They covered my head up and I was supposed to be asleep but I made this little peephole in the cloth and I could see out. I remember peeking out and seeing parts of things, parts of masks. I remember pretending to be asleep whenever they looked at me. That's sort of the way I grew up, always pretending to do what I was supposed to do, but not doing it. That was the beginning of my fantasy world, which is very important, I think, in being an artist. You have to be where you aren't."

Hardin's first important kachina painting, *Winter Awakening of the O-Khoo-Wah,* won the top prize at the Scottsdale National Indian Art Competition in 1972. The artist called it "very forceful and a bit contrived," a fair summation. "It said what I wanted to say about kachinas at the time, which is that they can be seen as Almighty Authority." After claiming the Scottsdale award, one of the most prestigious in Southwestern art, "I was in shock for a long time. I couldn't do anything. I didn't know how I could measure up to that one painting. Then I did *Return of the Cloud People,* also in 1972, which had a wonderful freedom." The English translation of O-Khoo-Wah is "Cloud People"; all kachinas en route to the earth are thus Cloud People, regardless of their individual identities. "These guys are still coming in on the clouds," Hardin said of the two spirits. "They are breaking through a rainbow." The artist applied the mottled multicolored background, the watery blue sky and the buttery yellow sunlight, with an atomizer and then turned her attentions to the robes (*mantas*) and headdresses (*tablitas*) of the kachinas, where complicated configurations of sacred accoutrements—evergreens are worn as symbols of eternal life, for example—were combined with original design elements that recalled motifs common to the Haida

Watermelon Break, 1978

Winter Awakening the O-Khoo-Wah, 1972

Indians of British Columbia.

Like many of Hardin's ostensible influences, the Haida designs were coincidences—she had not at that juncture explored the art of the Pacific Northwest. On the green tablita of the larger figure is a round shape peppered with tiny dots; arranged above it are other dots with tails, spermatazoic shapes. Hardin was asked on several occasions if the large shape might be an ovum and if the smaller shapes were in fact sperm. She always chuckled. "Any interpretation is fine with me. But they are traditional symbols—the large ball with the little dots is symbolic of water and the smaller figures are tadpoles, used in ancient Indian art as another water symbol. Prehistoric Indians didn't have access to microscopes; I don't think they knew what sperm looked like." Another painting, *Arrival of Winter Messengers* (1981), of three nearly interchangeable kachinas, called forth this response, to Hardin's delight, from one of her collectors, Mary McClure: "They look to me like they're all going to run off and sing 'doo wop' behind the pueblo. Either that, or they've gotten dressed up so they can go down to the road and tell the Truth."

The kachina series continued through the seventies and into the eighties while other variations on other themes—robed figures, eagles, assorted animals—were explored, exploited and came to natural ends. "I can't imagine not doing kachinas," Hardin commented. "These are real spiritual people in my world. They're universal and godlike. There's an infinite variety. And they are like normal people, in that each one is an individual. I have a tendency to do my important kachina pictures with feathers and evergreens in the wintertime, not in the summer, which is out of cycle with when they are on earth—they are supposed to arrive around Easter and be present until late August—but it's my own world, so why not? I don't worry about who they are. As long as they're real to me when I'm doing them, that's enough."

Kachinas can be compared to the human population they serve in other respects, too: speaking philosophically, they are caught between two worlds, between heaven and earth—Hardin invariably painted them as Cloud People—and are thus in a state of perpet-

ual suspension. They are the artist's conscious vision of God, her unconscious vision of man. And of woman: with the arrival of her magnificent "Women Series" in 1980, the connection for Hardin between kachinas and humanity, and between kachinas and Hardin herself, would be clarified.

Pablita Velarde was frankly mystified by her daughter's utilization of sacred material. "She's gone and got into this real contemporary thing. It's a little bit way out for my level. Where I'm so traditional in lots of ways, she's so far out in space, sometimes I don't know what it's all about. If it appeals to me, I tell her so, but I don't understand it. She has studied in her own way the kachinas, and from there she begins in her own mind to create things. I suppose it's all right, but it doesn't represent anything of true significance to the pueblo, except that it's a mask. You can't identify which kachina it is because it's in Helen's head."

That was for public dissemination. After her daughter's death, Velarde privately told Hardin's husband, "Helen may have got cancer because she painted kachinas." Cradoc Bagshaw was less horrified than saddened by the accusation; he had come to terms with Pueblo religion, and had a theory as to why Hardin never practiced it except in its most spiritual form. "Of course, she was rejected, that was it in the beginning, but I could see that the religion itself had also deteriorated. It is a secret religion: I've compared it to the Catholic Church during the Inquisition, when people practically got sick on their own power. Here's an example. Helen and I went up to visit the pueblo for a night and we were warned by Aunt Jane not to look outside. I don't know why the incident itself happened, but I think it may have had something to do with a purification ceremony, because Aunt Jane's son was in an accident, though that's all theory on my part, and I couldn't get any explanation from Helen. She wasn't at liberty to say. Anyway, there were noises all night. And this much I know: outside all night there were people who were supposed to be 'bear people' from Jemez Pueblo, the idea being that there are middle people, between animal and human, who can be used for certain things, but the inheritance ran out at Santa Clara, so when they need them, they

*Arrival of Winter
Messengers,* 1981

bring them in from another pueblo. They were guys from Jemez eating rags and then throwing them up; this is typical behavior.

"There are two points to this story. One, Helen was furious that they'd told her not to look outside: 'I'm as much a part of this pueblo as anyone,' she said, but of course she wasn't. As long as I knew her, she'd say, 'They always count me in when they want money from the government, they count me in for the census, but then they try to keep me away from everything.' The second point is that Helen bypassed the bullshit of a decadent religion and communicated directly with her gods. The religion itself became secret because of the Spanish—they would cut off Indians' feet for doing religious dances. So, like any secret religion, it got out of hand. I think it started as a noble religion but the practice of it now can be quite disgusting. You can make an analogy to the U.S. Constitution, which is a wonderful guide, but is ignored in practice. The *Book of the Hopi* is a nonsecret guide to a secret religion, which is why you won't find discussions of witchcraft in it, even though there are all kinds of women in the pueblos who think they are witches. Pablita was afraid of all this, and believed in it, and that's why she actually thinks the pueblo had the power to kill her daughter for making pictures."

The impetus in the major kachina paintings was toward greater size and abstraction, but not necessarily simplification. *Night of the O-Khoo-Wah* (1980) is a highly intricate structure that is unexpectedly playful, a kind of kachina highrise. (It contains a subliminal joke. Turned upside down, the eyes and mouths of many of the figures continue to read in relation to each other as faces, as if right side up. "It's a little game I was playing with myself," Hardin said.) Three years later, *Voices of Thunder,* as monumental as *Night of the O-Khoo-Wah* is whimsical, was completed; this time, the colors are highly saturated and the application of the airbrush is aggressive—there are sections of the painting that have been sprayed with tiny red dots that hint at spattered blood. The two overlapping masks are obviously kachinas, but their individual identities have been all but subsumed by the cropping of the composition. "These are Cloud People again," Hardin said. "Their song on the way to the earth is thunder.

Night of the O-Khoo-Wah, 1980

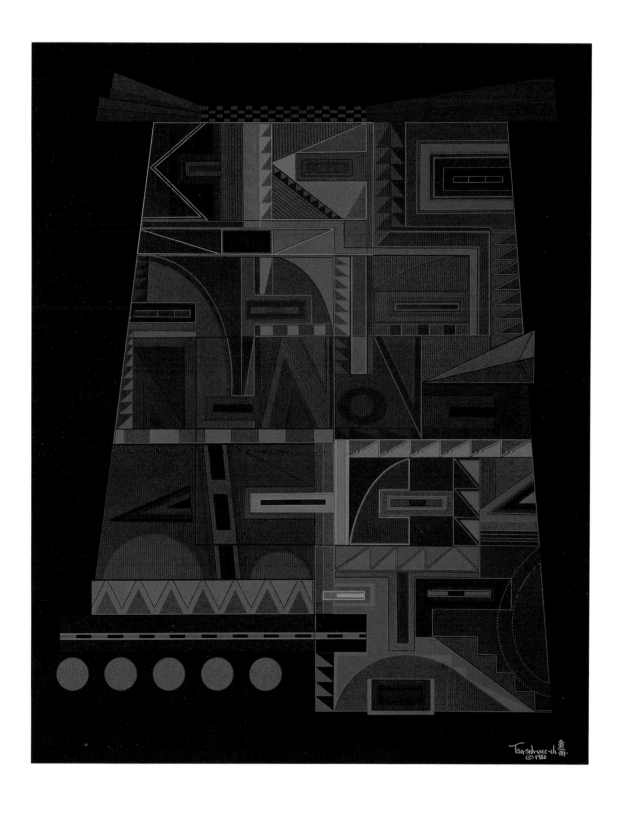

They are almost abstract; I really like abstract painting, but I like the spiritual element too. I think all my paintings have to have something alive in them. You can make clouds alive, but some designs you can't make alive. Some things stay things."

Hardin's few abstracts—*Casas Grandes Polychrome* (1977), for instance—were less successful. "I did that as an experiment," she conceded. The motifs were adapted from polychrome pottery unearthed near Chihuahua, Mexico, at Casas Grandes, the largest prehistoric Indian community in the Southwest, and Hardin was curious to see if "they could look good as a painting." Not especially: the decorative forms, divorced from the sensual curves of the pottery and with nothing to decorate, are inert; Hardin's organization of them follows the logic of spatial expediency. She redeemed her interest in the Casas Grandes designs in 1982 with a complicated and mechanistic work painted on a piece of the watercolor board she preferred to canvas. She had primed the board in black. Thinking that she might do an abstract, she began painting at the lower left corner and moved out, knitting familiar forms together in unfamiliar ways, until a face appeared, absolutely unbidden, in the center. The colliding angles recall Joseph Stella's Futurist painting of the twenties, *New York Interpreted V: The Bridge* (1922), but again the influence is coincidence, and there is nothing in the machine-age movement of the twenties to account for the symbology of the circle of golden glaze that harmonizes Hardin's otherwise apparently arbitrary, dissonant composition, and there are no forms in mainstream American art that correspond to the feather fan that flourishes, like an obscenely sensual beard, below the figure's halolike chin. To Hardin, who had been ill with cancer for more than a year at the time, the painting was an unsettling apparition, an unpredictable kachina that had lost its beneficence, a portrait of a thing that was living but perhaps not alive. "*Metamorphosis* was human, it was organic," she declared. "I'm not sure what this is." She called the picture *Vision of Darkness* and was not sorry when it was sold.

Voices of Thunder, 1983

Casas Grandes Polychrome, 1977

Vision of Darkness, 1982

Medicine Talk, casein 1964

FIVE
A Total Double Life

The photograph snapped to publicize Hardin's first "formal" one-woman show at Enchanted Mesa in 1964 is a pretty little thing of a pretty little thing. Hardin, clad in traditional Pueblo garb, is arranged decorously in front of three paintings: a stylized study of a plant form indebted to her mother's work, and two stupifyingly clichéd caseins of Indian children. *Medicine Talk* (1964), the one painting in the show that would prove significant to Hardin's career, is nowhere in evidence, nor is the artist's state of mind—a mixture of confusion, fear, anger and determination. The confusion was over her past; the fear was for her future; the anger was a function of her situation; and the determination was a naked survival instinct. "I was treated like a cute little Indian girl—so sweet, so beautiful. People would say, 'Here are these *precious* paintings, we've just got to have one, and you know, they're *only* twelve dollars!' The show came about because I was going to make a lot of money from the paintings and run away from home. I was three months pregnant. Nobody knew. It was my secret. I made a little money but not enough. I couldn't leave. I was stuck."

The idyllic childhood had been shattered when Velarde informed her children their father was having an affair with another woman. At first, Hardin thought her mother must be mad, must be making it up. "I didn't want to believe anything bad about my dad. He was a very gentle, very nice, very quiet person, always so nice to us. But it was true. He had found another woman who reached him on a mutual level. She was a cop, he was a cop, and after he left my mom, they got married. I think my mother made life hard for my father—she's a very controlling person—and when the going got rough, he left. I took it hard." Velarde concurred with her daughter's version of events. "Helen was really hurt. She was his favorite. We had been married fifteen years but only lived together about seven. He left when Helen was thirteen. Until then, she'd had no cares in the world. Then she took her feelings out on everyone. I don't know

*Helen and her brother Herby,
this photograph was taken circa
1959, when Helen and Herby
were both in high school.*

how patient I was at the time. Maybe not too patient." Under the
circumstances, patience for Velarde was all but impossible, and
because her anger at her husband was so intractable and uncontrollable, she saw her daughter's grief as an unmanageable irritation. As
late as Christmas of 1983, Velarde refused to discuss her ex-husband.
"I don't want nothing to do with that man," she snapped. "I liked his
sister, though, and I went to her funeral last month. I saw him there.
He lives in Arizona now, he's an assistant warden at a minimum
security prison. I didn't say anything to him. I just looked at him
from a distance. I said to Helen, 'Keep him out of my way.'"

"My father," Hardin added, "waved to my mom. He has no
desire to be negative to her. I took him into the chapel. Other relatives took my mom in. I had signed the guest register, my dad had
signed after me. My mom made the relatives she was with sign first,
so her name wouldn't be next to his. Then she sat way in the back,
to be the first to leave."

Hardin's rebelliousness could not be attributed solely to her
father's absence; like her mother, she had been what feminists in the
seventies would call "her own person" almost from infancy. Think-

Helen's graduation from St. Pius X (1961) meant that she had to decide what to do with her life: college and marriage seemed to be her choices.

ing back on her night in the kiva when she was four years old, she remembered asking her brother if he had also peeked. "No," he replied, "they told me to go to sleep. So I did." Hardin thought the behavior typical—of both siblings. "Herby always minded my mom. If she told me to go to sleep, I'd wonder why she wanted me to, and then would stay up to find out. In my adolescence, after my father left, my mother was very strict with me, but if she told me not to go to a dance, I'd jump out the window and go. I was in Catholic school, St. Pius X in Albuquerque, so there was very heavy control there, too, but at school the nuns loved me. I would smoke in the bathroom with the girls who *were* bad, but I was still one of the rah-rahs, the clique that had the shining apples for the teachers. I really didn't like the wonderful *A* student group and the cheerleaders, I enjoyed being with the others. I was always going from one group to the other, I thought *everybody* had to like me, the good guys had to like me, the bad guys had to like me, and I wanted *all* the boys to like me. But I wouldn't go so far as to jeopardize anything: I didn't get laid until after I graduated from high school. There were girls getting laid, even in Catholic school—there were girls who were pregnant

when they graduated. A third of our class got married the first week after graduation. That was their vocation.

"Everyday I would pray for my vocation. I got panic-stricken about February and told the priest I didn't know what I would do when I graduated. He said, 'Say a Hail Mary every day and pray for your vocation,' and I did, but I still didn't know what I was going to do. All I could think of was to go to college and find someone to marry. That's how we were programmed. I didn't plan to make pictures. I always did art in high school and got good feedback—Helen was *the* artist, and when we decorated for the prom or needed posters, it was me—but there was the problem with my mother. She was in her prime then, always in the newspapers. Everyone thought I would be an artist, too, but I was rebelling against my mother in a serious way. I did spend the summer of my junior year in a special art class for Indians held by the University of Arizona, but I asked to be transferred to the weaving section—I enjoyed that, working with pure design—because I had already learned how to do the stuff, por-traits and landscapes, they were teaching the reservation Indians. People always asked me if I would be an artist like my mother and I always said yes, but in my last year in high school, I thought, I'm going to be an actress, I'm going to paint somebody's nails, *anything* but be an artist. It's funny. When I started the University of New Mexico in the fall, I took art history and courses in design, drawing and anthropology, but I still told myself I was not going to be an artist. When she wasn't trying to get me to go into business, my mother was insistent that I was going to stay in Albuquerque, become an artist and marry an Indian. Marry an Indian? Yuk. That's exactly what I thought. All my mother's life she hated His-panics, so of course the first thing I did in college was to start going out with Hispanic football players. It just seemed the right thing to do; and the bigger the better. I went out with Bobby Santiago first, and then with Pat Terrazas. He was very attractive, he knew how to dance—I loved to dance—and he knew enough slimy bartenders so he could get me into nightclubs underage. We won dance contests and I was getting great attention; I decided I was going to be a dancer, too. I stayed at the University of New Mexico one year, and then went to visit my father in Washington, D.C., where he was working for USAID. I thought I would go to the big city and get a job and get my own apartment. I didn't. I lived with my father and worked as a file clerk with a woman who sneered at the 'damn niggers' every time a handsome African in an incredibly beautiful robe went by. When it started raining, I came home. It started raining in late October of 1962. I asked my dad how long it lasted and he said, 'I don't know, all winter, I guess.' I came home, lived with my mom and she put me in business college. She thought I could get a good job as a secretary. I started seeing Pat again.

"I was lost. I didn't want to do anything. I [sold] children's dresses and I had jobs as a waitress. And I had Pat. That was getting real messy. He was mean and musclebound and threatened to kill me if I saw anyone else. My mom didn't like him and he didn't like her and I didn't like either one of them. It was horrible. Finally I didn't paint at all. When I had painted at home, my mom's criticism was not constructive and since it brought on more bad feelings, I stopped. It was no better when I moved in with Pat, but I did do art again. While he was at work, I would sneak out my paints. I used casein, so it wasn't imperative that I keep them wet; I had a little flat watercolor pan I could shove under the dresser real fast when he came home; I'd put the paintings behind the dresser and stick the brushes in my drawer; he'd open the door and I'd be in front of the television set looking...uninteresting. That's how he wanted me. He didn't want me painting because he didn't like the attention I got, and he thought if I didn't paint I wouldn't have an excuse to go out."

Hardin and Terrazas lived not far from Enchanted Mesa. "Those were terrible years for Helen," Margarete Chase said. "She would come in with bruises on her face. He gave them to her." Fred and Margarete Chase, married forty-nine years in 1985, were legends among Indian traders for the quality of the Indian artifacts they sold and for the fairness with which they treated their "Indian friends." The Chases met Pablita Velarde at an Inter-Tribal Indian Ceremonial in Gallup in the early fifties and sold her work steadily; in 1956, the year of Velarde's divorce, they became her exclusive representatives. "Pablita came over one day with a friend," Mrs. Chase recollected. "She was so blue. We suggested giving her a show. That really started something. I don't know how many shows we've had for her since. And then we started giving Helen shows, too."

The first "formal" show, in 1964, was possible because Hardin had yet to move in with Terrazas; she was still living with her mother. When her escape failed and when she had given birth on Nov. 11, 1964, to her daughter, Margarete (named after Mrs. Chase), and when the situation with her mother had became intolerable, she reluctantly acquiesced to Terrazas's requests that they become a family. "At least I had a lot of time alone," Hardin laughed ruefully. "He was always selling cars, or spending time in a bar, or spending the night somewhere else. I had my own place, sort of, except this man would come in to change his clothes and beat me up. He was connected in some way with organized crime. I kept painting secretly. Things had to change."

The 1964 show gave Hardin some confidence in her ability. *Medicine Talk,* with its curvilinear smoke and swirling robes and asexual proto-psychedelic tone, was a tentative step away from the traditional work of her mother—the painting is a genre scene, but there is no narrative. "Traditional painting tells a story," Hardin said in interviews in the sixties. "Modern painting leaves you with a feeling. I am a modern painter." Nonetheless, she was receiving commissions to do conventional paintings—the patron would point to an earlier work and say, "Just like that one"—and she was unwaveringly obliging. "I was everybody's good little girl, but I was angry about it, every minute I was doing it." Several observers told her that her most experimental forays reminded them of other non-Indian artists, but she didn't know who they were talking about. "I only knew I was being compared to someone who was dead and famous. I thought that was neat."

Hardin now longed to investigate art history and fantasized taking art classes, but she had other, more pressing priorities. The career Terrazas knew nothing about was well under way. "Pat would let me

Passport photograph, taken in 1968; Helen and daughter Margarete were on their way to Colombia.

go visit Margarete Chase, because she was no threat, she was an old lady. She would tell me she had a speaking engagement for me, I would go over to Enchanted Mesa in my jeans, change at her place, go give a talk—once it was to the Children of the American Revolution—and then change and go home. It was a total double life and it was making me a little crazy." Hardin's father had, in the meantime, been transferred to Colombia, where he was to set up a program to train local police officers, and he agreed vigorously when his daughter wrote and asked if she could visit for an extended period, as a way of liberating herself from both Terrazas and her mother. Under her daughter's direction, Velarde had long been depositing in an Española, New Mexico, bank money earned from the secret painting sales; Hardin withdrew it, hid her luggage in a locker, and arranged for her mother to take her to the airport the next day. By the time Terrazas arrived at Velarde's home to inquire after Hardin, she was on her way to Miami with a tiny child who informed passengers that her name was Margarete and that she was going to Bogota by way of "Your-ami." Hardin would return six months later with a determination to keep Terrazas out of her life; more importantly, she would return with new ambitions and a new vision: the compliant illustrator skilled at genre scenes such as *San Geronimo Day at Taos* (1967), with its potbellied koshare kiddies evocative in equal measure of Brueghel and Hallmark, never came home.

Chief's Robes, casein 1968

SIX

Tsa-Sah-Wee-Eh Does Her Thing

T he shy but garishly made-up Indian girl in the Priscilla Presley beehive, the Native American *artiste* engineered to sell inexpensive paintings of endearing Indian children and cuddly animals, vanished when the March/April issue of *New Mexico Magazine* hit the newsstands in 1970. The United States was in Vietnam, the campuses of the country were in open revolt, and the counterculture's adoption of the wisdom of the American Indian was nearing its zenith. Albuquerque, Taos and Santa Fe were jammed with long-haired seekers after the Truth; dog-eared copies of *Book of the Hopi* were apt to be found next to a patchouli incense stick and a baggie full of dope in backpacks of compleat hippies. The photograph of Hardin that graced the cover of *New Mexico Magazine* above a caption of pristine sixties-speak — "Tsa-Sah-Wee-Eh Does Her Thing" — was a tailor-made pinup for the groovy groupie, and it did indeed take its place on commune walls, next to postery icons of the three graces of the pop revolution, Jane and Joan and Janis.

"That magazine turned the whole world around for me," Hardin said. "Everyone wanted a painting by Helen Hardin. It was insane. Everyone wanted jewelry like I was wearing. A woman married to an art dealer wanted a Pueblo haircut like mine; there were lots of women who wanted to look like me. I thought I looked real with-it on that cover, in front of Puyé Cliffs, but I was amazed when Fred and Margarete told me there were people coming into Enchanted Mesa wanting to buy a painting, wanting to buy the necklace, the earrings, the concha belt — they wanted the whole Helen Hardin kit. I could have cashed in on it, if I'd been smart, but I've never been able to think like that. The magazine came out and I got kidney stones and was sent to the hospital. When the *Albuquerque Tribune* sent a photographer around to get my reaction, they took a picture of me in my hospital bed."

The publicity fortuitously coincided with the expansive period in Hardin's art that had begun two years earlier with her return from

The cover that started it all; after this issue appeared, interest in Helen and her work soared. (Courtesy New Mexico Magazine*)*

Colombia. *New Mexico Magazine's* article, a gushy profile, carried a reproduction of *Chief's Robes,* which had been painted in 1968 and won first prize "for innovation" at the 1969 Inter-Tribal Indian Ceremonial. That it could be considered innovative at a time when Happenings and Warhol and Minimalism were firmly entrenched in New York could be seen as indicative of the backwardness of Indian art, perhaps, but also of its refusal to relinquish its regionalism, a refusal that Hardin would one day put to profitable use: because she was blithely ignorant of the ground that had been covered in the East, she was fearless when it came to following well-travelled routes, and thanks to the untrained freshness of her vision, the sights she saw seemed new. She had already incorporated the Native art (known as "primitive" in those days) that had given inspiration to artists as diverse as Jackson Pollock, Max Ernst and Martha Graham; she had absorbed it so utterly that when she was exposed to the work of Picasso, with whom she might have been expected to feel an affinity, she was unmoved. "It took me a long time to appreciate him," she said. "I couldn't figure out what he was doing. It seemed to have nothing to do with me. It still doesn't, but of course I admire him."

Chief's Robes impressed the Gallup judges as innovative because it looked nothing at all like the paintings of Pablita Velarde and looked even less like the paintings they had come to expect from her daughter; nor did it resemble the art of other young Indians. There was no attempt at the ethnographic reportage so beloved by white patrons: the men could have belonged to any tribe, or to none. The chiefs were in fact *designed,* rather than rendered naturalistically—they were no more and no less animate than the robes whose contours their facial features echoed, or the curls of smoke that emanated from their bonfire. They held in their hands not some television fantasy of a Noble Savage's ever-present peace pipe, but mundane store-bought or roll-your-own cigarettes that might well have been joints. Although Hardin herself did not smoke marijuana, *Chief's Robes* intentionally combined Indian communalism and a suggestion of ritual drug-taking so as to evoke, with the barest of whispers, its contemporary counterculture counterpart. But if the forms appeared to be psychedelic, the appearance was deceptive: the designs behind the chiefs were derived from the pottery of antiquity, and the spatter, splatter and stippling techniques Hardin employed to integrate background and foreground were prompted by similar harmonizing strategies in the Anasazi pottery found at Sikyatki and Awatobi. The equal emphasis Hardin allotted—and would continue to allot, throughout her career—to the animate and the ostensibly inanimate was also a product of a distinctively Native perception. Inculcated in the minds of most Pueblo and Hopi Indians is an ecological consciousness of extraordinary amplitude that sees the universe, in the words of *Book of the Hopi,* as "a web of relationships that includes not only all the societies of man, but all the sub-orders of the plant and animal kingdoms, the super-orders of spiritual beings, and the living entities of the earth and the stars above. None of them is alone and free to act independently. They are all interrelated in a web of correlative obligations and must function harmoniously for the perpetuation and progression of all on that one cosmic Road of Life." Hence the apparent compositional clutter, by Western standards, of *Recurrence of Spiritual Elements* is mandated by the subject, and by the pan-

Recurrence of Spiritual Elements, 1973

theistic nature of Pueblo religion. Had Hardin read Kandinsky, she would have understood precisely what he meant when he wrote, "The impact of the acute angle of a triangle on a circle is actually as overwhelming in effect as the finger of God touching the finger of Adam in Michelangelo."

Not only was *Chief's Robes* a general indication of things to come, it was the specific prototype for a fruitful series of robed figures, a series that began promisingly, continued respectably and sometimes spectacularly and ended appropriately, exactly at the moment when degeneration into the purely and merely decorative loomed as inevitable. There were robed figures standing side-by-side, robed figures intertwined, single robed figures and figures whose robes were beside the point. "For a long time, the more I did them, the more I saw I could do with them," Hardin said. "But when someone asked me to do another, after I had stopped, I found all the creativity had gone out of it. It was drudgery; I hate turning something I love into drudgery." At its conclusion, the series had accounted for at least seven major paintings and innumerable smaller studies, and had engendered a cottage industry of imitators—"When other artists started copying them, I called the last one *The Original Robes* (1980) and went on to other things"—but the formally worked-out overlaps perfected in the Day-Glo robed figures would overlap much of Hardin's ouevre.

In the remarkable kachina trinity painting of 1983, *Guardians of Infinity*, the two series, kachina and robe, meld. The painting consists of some twenty-five layers of iridescent acrylic overlaid with gold dust in a crystalline acrylic base; the layers and the juxtapositions of contrasting color contrive to provide a playful now-you-see-it, now-you-don't, three-dimensionality usually absent in Hardin's work. The planes proceed into the viewer's space and immediately recede, depending on where the eye chooses to wander. Nothing in this painting is what it seems. Ambient lighting and the placement of the spectator contribute to the shifting illusion: a tiny alteration in illumination induces a change in the relationship of the planes; a slight movement by the viewer to either side of the frame frees light to

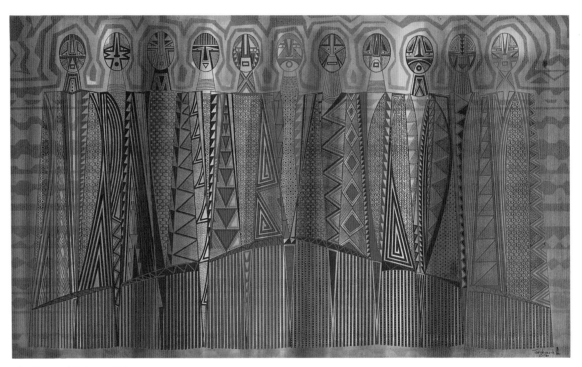

The Original Robes, 1980

strike the metallic flecks in unpredictable patterns, resulting in wildly varying color intensities; and from several angles, the image is actually buried in a smooth, featureless expanse of opaque, glistening gold. The game that is being played here owes allegiance to the rules of Op art, certainly, but the optical illusion, which is neither complete nor consistent, is metaphysical in orientation. The three kachinas are paradoxes, at one with each other yet separate, three-dimensional yet confined to a single plane—they are representations of a world view that recognizes individual attributes but finds the whole to be more than the sum of the parts. Jungian aesthetician Aniele Jaffe has said, "a true symbol appears when there is a need to express what thought cannot think." *Guardians of Infinity* is a symbol of the sophisticated theological concept of a multifaceted but all-encompassing deity: the trinity made flesh (or at least iridescent geometry).

Guardians of Infinity, 1983

Plumed Serpent of the Singing Waters, 1977

*Old Age Brings Visions of
Rainbows,* 1976

Hardin's fascination with robes and with metallic acrylics—she bought her first tube in 1976, and felt it had been manufactured especially for her—led to two self-confessed experiments in the application of the sparkling, neon-esque liquids, *Old Age Brings Visions of Rainbows* (1976), and *Robed in Rainbows* (1976); of the former, Hardin observed, "It might be just as good a painting if I had left the face out and you had a pile of abstract shapes, a pyramid. The other painting was an experiment in applying paint by brush. Iridescents are much easier to control in an airbrush. I did layer after layer on his robes with a regular brush, and it was beautiful in its intensity, but it doesn't say anything." One of the most ravishing of the iridescent études is the black-on-black *Plumed Serpent of the Singing Waters* (1977). The Indian name for Santa Clara is Ka'Po: the title of Hardin's painting is the English translation of that sacred Tewa designation, hidden for centuries from the hated Spanish. The deity depicted is Avanyu, a water-carrier whose efforts are greeted with either joy or, in the case of flash floods, dread, and who is acknowledged ambivalently by all Pueblo peoples. Hardin employed this ancient serpent, thought to be related anthropologically to the Aztecs' Quetzacoatl, as a vehicle for a technical tour de force: the watercolor board was sprayed with silver until it took on the dusky sheen of pewter. "Then I put layers and layers and layers of pewter spray over that, and finished it off with another silver spray." Although black, the effulgent background all but undulates; once the solid serpent had been applied in matte black, he seemed to slither sinuously across the surface of the picture, an ebony snake dancing on an obsidian lake powdered in moondust. Yet again, Hardin had integrated figure and ground in a fashion that was technically progressive and philosophically meaningful. Her aversion to the commercial imperatives of art—her refusal to think in terms of markets and patrons—was evinced by her continued use of iridescents, which are glorious in a gallery but rarely wear well in reproduction. *Winter Sun Wears a Snowflake Veil* (1980) is draped in a silver shimmer that provides a lacy snowflake effect absent in photographs. "Iridescents turn to the nearest shade in photographs," Hardin sighed. "The coppers turn red, the golds become yellow and the silvers are gray."

Hardin priced *Chief's Robes* at $200, was informed she was charging too much, and wound up keeping the painting for herself. "When *New Mexico Magazine* came out," she laughed, surprised at the vestigial bitterness years later, "lots of people wanted it but I wouldn't sell it. I had been told, 'My dear, you're just getting started.' I think that's always the penalty you pay for being young: you're treated as an inferior thing, as if you have no feelings and haven't paid any dues. I was twenty-five by the time I painted *Chief's Robes*. I'd paid a lot of dues." Neither *Chief's Robes* nor *Petroglyph* (1968), one of a number of quasi bas-reliefs based on rock drawings Hardin had sketched at the ruins of San Cristobal Pueblo (abandoned in the wake of the Great Pueblo Rebellion), was typical of her Enchanted Mesa output, which remained largely faithful to The Studio style. *Petroglyph,* thick with simulated impasto (the medium was acrylic paste), presented abstracted caterpillars climbing cornstalks, the Hopi swastika (symbolic of the migrations of the Hopi people, and of the movements of the earth and the sun) and the spiral of life in an environment as raw and unschooled as the source. The prehistoric iconography had been consumed, but not digested. In the early eighties, Hardin returned again to petroglyphs, this time as a mature artist in full command of her vision; the images were now an inseparable part of her art. In the elegant shadow painting *Ghosts on Canyon Walls* (1981), patterned after a mysterious godlike representation

Winter Sun Wears a Snowflake Veil, 1980

Hardin found scratched on a California cliff, and in *Arrow Swallow Ceremony* (1982), a small single-line jewel that again incorporates the spiral of life and that embeds the figure in a loosely composed but densely complex background of grainy inkwash—the overlay paint was mixed with sand—there is an unswerving belief in the ability of properly presented ancient images to engineer timeless epiphanies. (Pueblo and Hopi Indians offhandedly discuss dreams and symbolism as if they had been reading the more speculative works of Jung, psychiatrist Robert Coles reported in *Eskimos, Chicanos, Indians,* volume 4 of *Children of Crisis.*) The iconography of artists out of memory is magically communicated out of time: the paintings eerily transform modern walls into the sides of pre-Columbian caves, into slabs of rock bearing talismans and totems, potent symbols glimpsed dimly, as if through flickering firelight.

The 1968 petroglyph studies and *Chief's Robes* were executed not long after Hardin and Margarete returned from Colombia. The trip was notable for resulting in the first professional acclaim Hardin could be certain was untainted by respect for her mother: in her resumé for many years thereafter, the exhibition organized in Bogota by the American cultural attaché was listed as her first one-woman show, formal or otherwise. The attaché had visited Hardin's father, had been impressed by the daughter's work, and had arranged with her, on her arrival, to "paint like crazy"—there were some twenty-six pictures in the show, the majority traditional at the attaché's request ("He said the only thing Colombians knew about Indians came from the movies, and could I be educational as well as artistic?"), and all were received with warmth. "Everything sold, but about six paintings. It was wonderful. No one knew who I was, or who my mother was. They just liked my art and they liked me. I decided when I got back to the States I would have my own apartment, my own car and my own art. My own life."

She produced exclusively for the Chases and lived frugally ("We ate a lot of hamburger") in a $65-a-month apartment. "Fred and Magarete were dependable. I turned out paintings and they bought everything and kept me alive for $250 a month." The notoriety that

Petroglyph, 1968

Ghosts on Canyon Walls, 1981

accrued to her from the *New Mexico Magazine* article was not reflected (and would not be, until 1974) in the prices of her paintings, which continued to be sold, on the low end, for fifty dollars. Hardin refused to see Terrazas but she did permit him to visit Margarete on neutral territory. Because she feared his volatile nature, she kept the whereabouts of her apartment a secret. "I never told Margarete our address or phone number. She was only four and if she had got lost, it would have been a disaster, but I couldn't tell her, because I knew he'd trick her and show up on my door. We hid out from him a couple of years. He gave me nothing, no child support. My mom always said to take him to court. I refused." Hardin married Cradoc Bagshaw in 1973, but Terrazas continued to pester her, until Bagshaw threatened to take him to court for past child support. Hardin's next and last awareness of Terrazas came in September of 1975 when she read, with a mixture of relief and sadness, that he had been shot through the head in the parking lot of the El Cid Nightclub and Lounge in a killing, intimated by the news accounts in the Albuquerque papers to be Mafia-related.

"My most vivid recollection of those years," Margarete said in 1985 at the age of twenty-one, "was my dad beating my mom. My very first memory of anything—I must have been about three years old—is of him coming home while she was watching television and punching her in the mouth. He chipped her tooth and she couldn't afford to have it fixed until 1974. I also remember him coming in when she was watching John Davidson, the singer. He asked her if she thought Davidson was 'cute.' When she said, 'Yes, I guess so,' he kicked her in the stomach and she blacked out on the floor. He treated me lovingly and I suppose he spoiled me: he was always there when I needed a little money or clothes."

From time to time, as Terrazas would discover Hardin's hideout, mother and daughter would be forced to move; from time to time, they moved back in with Pablita Velarde. "That was no better," Margarete said. "Pablita was drinking a lot in those days, at least a fifth of bourbon every night, and she'd started buying the half-gallon size. She beat my mom a lot. One night, my mom was putting hairpins in her hair. My grandmother asked her if she was going out. My mom said she wasn't. My grandmother kept at it—I think she called her a slut—and Pablita pulled the towel rack off the wall and hit Mom over the back of the head with it and then dragged her around the room. When I went to the mortuary to dress my mom after she'd died of cancer, I brought a wig with me to help make her look presentable, and I could still see the scar from the towel rack on her head. I was eleven when Dad died. He was shot by someone he'd beat up earlier. We heard it was because the guy owed somebody debts on an illegal poker game. My dad was always telling people he was one of 'the sons of Italy,' but he wasn't Italian—he meant he was connected in some way with the Mafia. The police knew who'd killed him, but the guy somehow covered his tracks, and I don't think the police ever pursued it. I think their attitude was, 'Good riddance.' My mom's reaction when Dad died was relief, because he was out of our lives. For me, it was really troubling. He wasn't a dad, really, but I called him that."

Had Terrazas not existed, the demands of motherhood and of her professional life would still have precluded Hardin's involvement in the alternative lifestyles of the era. "I was painting fifteen hours a day. But I was having fun—for the first time, I sought out friends who were in arts and crafts—even if I was very disciplined. I had to be careful because of Margarete. There was no way I was going to do acid and then have Margarete sitting around for three days wondering when I was going to come out of it. I had beer in my icebox and that was it." Although the *New Mexico Magazine* cover had made her an icon for radicals, she was divorced by her own temperament and training from their concerns. She did join the Vietnam War protest with a single gesture (her car headlights were illuminated on an appointed day) but she was otherwise apolitical, and she was downright unsympathetic to the American Indian Movement, the darling of many white liberals. Her reasons were complex. Hardin had known Russell Means, one of AIM's leaders, and found it impossible to take him seriously as a spokesman for Indian causes—she thought him fundamentally white, and she thought he and his colleagues had learned more philosophy from watching television than from tribal elders. Unlike many Indians, she had not been treated badly by whites, and she had been reared in a politically passive environment. Dr. Coles discovered that Pueblo and Hopi children were taught patience and tolerance in a manner suggestive of Kierkegaard's Christ, the suffering and fatalistic Christ who eventually triumphs through time and love: "If there are bad times as the result of what whites do, there is no cause to become excessively alarmed, unremittingly hateful; the world, as a whole, deserves too much respect for any segment of that world to be granted the ultimate authority that goes with fear or hate—or indeed efforts to conceal those emotions....Pueblo and Hopi children have been warned repeatedly that a consuming hate for the white man is evidence of the final subjection of the Indian." The Colombia trip had also reinforced Hardin's feelings: "I had come back," she said, "from a place where I had really seen Indians treated like shit; I had seen *people* treated like shit, children of prostitutes turned out at age three or four to make a living because the Catholic Church had told them that they could not use birth control. I was angry, but not at the white man. I was angry at the waste in America. I saw people, Indian and white, not taking advantage of what they had. I got very serious about taking advantage of what I had been given."

She was ready to protest, but only in paint. In 1970, she painted *Santa Clara Deer Dance,* one of her most accomplished acrylics in a traditional mode and one of her last.

SEVEN
Suspended In Heavenly Splendor.

Tonita Peña, the pioneering Pueblo artist whose nascent feminism provided a potent role model for Pablita Velarde, exerted her greatest influence on the future not through her own work, but through the curiously truncated career of her son, Joe H. Herrera. In the two most comprehensive surveys of Native art available in the early seventies—J.J. Brody's *Indian Painters & White Patrons* and Clara Lee Tanner's *Southwest Indian Painting*—Herrera was said to have been the prime mover in enlarging the syntax and sophistication of modern Indian painting. (Hardin, whose career had barely begun, was discussed in both volumes as a promising young woman deeply indebted to Herrera.) "The first Indian painter to shift successfully from the restricted vocabulary of Indian art to the White mainstream," Brody maintained of Herrera, and added that he made the shift "deliberately and intelligently and received a great deal of encouragement from the White world while doing so."

Herrera was instructed by his mother at home and was subsequently graduated from The Studio in 1940; he enrolled in art classes at the University of New Mexico in 1950, a year after Tonita Peña died, and was soon submerged in the work of Klee, Kandinsky and the Analytical Cubists by professor Raymond Jonson, a painter in his own right and a charter member of a loose aggregation of Southwestern artists known as "the transcendentalists," a movement that briefly included Georgia O'Keeffe and the Canadian landscape specialist Lawren Harris. Unlike Dorothy Dunn, Jonson felt that exposure to mainstream art would benefit Indians, and he encouraged Herrera to filter his Pueblo sensibilities through mainstream strategies. The result was so successful that Herrera was invited to exhibit at the Museum of Modern Art in New York. But he abruptly ceased painting in 1958 and confined himself to his job as a Santa Fe bureaucrat; he was, Brody believed, "acculturated but unassimilated," a victim who realized "the impossibility of being both a tribal Indian and an idiosyncratic painter" and was therefore "defeated by accultura-

Suspended in Heavenly Splendor, 1979

tion as were so many other tribal Indians who attempted to make their way in urban White settings." (The possibility that Herrera might simply have been a casualty of creative burnout, the potential plague of every artist, was, oddly enough, left undiscussed.)

Brody dubbed Herrera's followers "the modifiers" and noted that a "surprising number" were themselves the children of painters: "Among the most polished…are Tony Da of San Ildefonso, son of Popovi Da and grandson of Maria and Julian Martinez; Michael Kabotie of Hopi, son of Fred Kabotie; Tyler Polelonema, son of Otis Polelonema; and Helen Hardin, daughter of Pablita Velarde of Santa Clara.…All, however, were more strongly influenced by Herrera's paintings than by those of their parents." A decade later, that had changed. Writing of Hardin in the summer 1979 issue of *American Indian Art Magazine,* Kansas State University art history professor LouAnn Faris Culley observed that it was "inevitable" Velarde's daughter would be attracted to Herrera but argued that "it can be definitely established that Hardin has progressed far beyond her youthful enthusiasm for Herrera's art to create something that is her own. In matters of technique Hardin was influenced by Herrera, who was the first contemporary painter to use what was probably a prehistoric method of paint application—the spray or spatter. Undoubtedly Herrera's abstract presentation of ancient symbols found in Southwest rock art also dazzled the young Hardin, offering a contrast to the traditional styles of her mother and other American Indian artists whom she knew."

Both sources—the smoothly decorative arcane symbology of Herrera and the stylized genre scenes of The Studio—came together in *Santa Clara Deer Dance,* a painting that its owner, Fred Chase, invariably unveiled by saying, "If you ask me, this is the best thing Helen Hardin ever did. Wouldn't part with it." It *is* the best thing Helen Hardin ever did—in the style of Joe H. Herrera and The Studio. "I was still holding on to the traditional but trying to make it contemporary," Hardin said, critically scrutinizing a reproduction of the painting. "I hadn't made the break. This is stylized and it tells a story: the deer dancers are coming down from the mountain. End of

Santa Clara Deer Dance, 1970

story. Fred thought it was the best thing I've ever done, but so do some other collectors of Indian art, because they don't have to think about what it is. There's no challenge to it. Color-wise and in terms of composition, it's a good painting, but I'd never do it again. Never." Hardin had reached a turning point in 1970: there were no new depths for her to plumb in The Studio's clichés or in the initially hortatory art of Herrera. The dead-end was frighteningly visible in *Buffalo Dance* (date unknown), where the dancers had become so geometrically mannered they were like a Native American cartoon parody of cubism. The volumetric presentation was a departure from the customarily flat figures of The Studio, but in this case, Hardin's ignorance of mainstream art worked to her disadvantage: she was discovering the wheel in a world of starships. Her primary interest, she remarked years later, lay not in the figures, but in the background design, derived from a Pueblo kilt. "I would get into the design and then put figures in front, any kind of figures. Back then, I was going through a phase where I was attracted to pure design, even in humans or animals." The "spiritual element" that frequently guided her feelings was absent and did not return until "I had really had it with being my mother's daughter and thought I had to make a name for myself and had to be Helen Hardin. The article in *New Mexico Magazine* helped make it possible."

Velarde had a clear recollection of what Hardin consistently christened "the break": "We've kind of lived separate lives, my daughter and me—I don't even know who she studied with at the university, to tell you the truth, that's how much I know about my own daughter—but she didn't want to be referred to as Pablita's daughter after she moved away from home, and that's the way they always referred to her when we gave an art show together: 'This is Pablita, and this is Pablita's daughter, Helen.' She got tired of that. I don't blame her. I don't think I'd want to be someone else's shadow. She began to branch out and was strong enough to do it. I'm real proud of what she's doing, whatever it is."

What she was doing, as in *Father Sky Embracing Mother Earth* (1971), was transforming Indian myth into modern metaphor, a metaphor that could be deciphered—or, more properly, *felt*—without reference to Pueblo or Hopi mythology. Herrera had set out on a similar path but had ultimately gone astray. Citing *Petroglyphic Turtle* (1952) as his evidence, Brody systematically demolished Herrera's claims to having created a cross-cultural art. "The temptation is to read *Turtle* as a personal statement, symbolically meaningful, but symbolism is a tricky business....Where metaphor had been called for, Herrera had used specific symbols or iconographic elements that appeared to be specific symbols. They were visual cryptograms, requiring a code book in order to be understood, and instead of being 'interpretative of my culture' they simply become one more mystery to be solved by the outsider....The viewer then was left not knowing whether esoteric knowledge was necessary for an understanding of the paintings. To the degree that words are necessary to explain the meaning of a picture that is intended for a specific audience, then that picture is a failure; in that, Herrera failed." Mentioning neither Herrera nor Brody, but delivering a thinly disguised broadside against both, Culley argued in an intelligently laudatory 1981 article on Hardin, published in *Helicon Nine, A Journal of Women's Arts and Letters,* that Hardin had found the key to Herrera's conundrum:

> "As several writers have pointed out, prior to 1920, nonritual Indian paintings had emphasized decoration or description over symbolism to such an extent that it had resulted in severe intellectual limitations. Later, there were some who, perceiving the artist's role as that of interpreter, commentator or even philosopher, tried to overcome those limitations but only succeeded in putting themselves into intellectual predicaments they were never able to solve. Many critics have suggested the reason for their failure was that their symbols lacked iconographic significance for white viewers—that they had no public currency, no 'universality.' This was not really the problem, however, since none of the twentieth-century art that has its source in the self, surrealism, metaphysical art, or the non-objective art of Klee and Kandinsky, used symbols which had that kind of public cur-

rency. Artists such as Klee, Kandinsky, Ernst or Matta could, however, make a strong initial impact on the viewer and could then convince him that the painting was not simply a catalog of mysterious symbols which could be deciphered with the help of something outside the painting. Rather, if the viewer wishes to decipher the symbols, to unravel the mystery, he must look within the painting itself. Where others failed to convince the viewer that their paintings were this kind of metaphor, Hardin has succeeded."

Culley advised *Helicon Nine* readers to approach Hardin's art secure in the knowledge it "presupposes no knowledge on our part concerning Pueblo religion and its symbolism," that the paintings carry "a general spiritual message" and that although the iconography may be specific in its source for Hardin (or may not be, depending on the painting), her images "speak to anyone who has ever had a spiritual experience, evoking the deities not of any one religion but of all religions." In this connection it is intriguing to learn that when Hardin was painting *Father Sky Embracing Mother Earth,* the iconography functioned reflexively for her: she began the picture with a study of an eagle, bordered it with pre-Columbian pottery designs she modified intuitively (the Pueblo ceremonial colors red and green are not found in pottery) and added the kaleidoscopic geometric ball in the center only when she thought the space too large, "too empty," to be left alone; the final flourish was the poetic title. (The process sometimes worked in reverse. *Fathers and Sons of the Mimbres,* 1970, came about because a picture was needed to go with a title already in mind.) Hardin decided, revealingly, that the circle surrounded by the eagle, "was so complex it had to be a woman. The eagle automatically became Father Sky." Because she was not conscious of a spiritual index does not, of course, imply that it did not exist—her work frequently called upon a spirituality that might be operating unconsciously or automatically, and only later would the latent mysticism manifest itself; only later would she see that a painting was more spiritual, more related to Pueblo religious concepts, than she had at first supposed.

Father Sky Embracing Mother Earth, 1971

The one aspect of her work that was never allowed to lapse into reflex was the search for perfection, a search that could be traced through the many elaborations of the eagle that followed *Father Sky*. The technique Hardin had chosen to develop was awesomely complex and punishingly time-consuming, forcing her to work long hours to begin to approximate the output of a reasonably adept, routinely facile artist. The multitude of tiny, hairlike lines on *Father Sky* had been drawn arduously with a free hand, and while they were as evenly measured as the steadiest of arms could manage, Hardin remained unsatisfied with their appearance; she gratefully replaced the almost microscopic idiosyncracies of free-hand application with the measured, rigid regularity of an architect's template. Overall, the thrust was toward renditions that were starker, simpler and more imposingly dramatic, as befitted her slightly awed interpretation of the eagle, the sacred guardian of the sky in Pueblo and Hopi mythology. *Visions in Heavenly Flight* (1977) showcased the deity in an earthy palette, but the composition was, in all other respects, a display of rigorously rarefied, unearthly design. The gray-green, pewterized plumage of *Suspended in Heavenly Splendor* (1979) belonged to a body superficially less abstracted and far more static than the preceding studies, but within the graceful outlines of its feathery finery, the lines were in busy and sharply worried motion; the juxtaposition of placid aquas with unexpectedly acid reds added to the toothy, sawing dissonance. Pueblo and Hopi Indians believe that the eagle has access to the Sun Kachina, the representative of universal harmony, also known as The Creator (but not to be confused with the anthropomorphic One God of the Judeo-Christian tradition—the Indian apprehension of the spiritual innerspring of the universe is comparatively vague). That is why "prayer feathers" are essential in ceremonials—eagle feathers are the vehicles by which the desires of men may reach the ears of the Infinite. Hardin honored this belief in her 1980 etching *Messenger from the Sun*. The eagle's wings segué on the right into a reproduction of the prayer sticks, called *pahos,* used by medicinemen; the sticks are stylized stand-ins for actual feathers. The remaining wing is indicated solely by *pahos,*

Visions in Heavenly Flight, 1977

while the life-giving force of the sun is communicated economically via three petals circumscribed by the disc. The etching is unusual in its direct symbolism — Hardin's vision became less specifically symbolic as time went on — but care was nevertheless taken to ensure that the composition would "read" as a harmonious, evocative whole, regardless of the viewer's background.

Two other eagle paintings of merit were completed that same year, *Plumed Prayers* and *Sikyatki Vision.* The former is a revival of a Mimbres feather motif that had already been expropriated by Julian Martinez, husband of the potter Maria. His version, reproduced on countless feather plates and bowls decorated first by himself and later by his son, Popovi Da, and his grandson, Tony Da, were exquisitely attenuated — and thoroughly divorced from religious resonance. In *Plumed Prayers,* Hardin restored the identity of the eagle as the heavenly conduit of earthly desire by restoring the head — the Martinez family had decapitated the creature in the interests of symmetrical decoration — and in *Sikyatki Vision,* prompted by designs discovered at the Hopi ruin, she invoked the weight, the near-bondage, of the eagle's destiny: the bird advances toward the viewer (a function of the play-off between the black background and the arching, blood-red beak) while the feathers remain stiffly, firmly in place, captives of their own geometrical elegance. The series climaxed in 1981 with a display of astonishing compositional virtuosity, a beige-and-black sliver of a painting, *Heavenly Protector.* Here, only a brilliant turquoise band near the eagle's beak and its faded echo on the neck accent Hardin's orchestration of the cascading curves of the eagle's body. No other accent is required. "I didn't want to add, as I had in *Father Sky,* any other shapes. The relationship of the center to the outside seemed perfect. The emptiness seemed perfect. The lines were perfect, perfectly measured. Everything was in harmony."

The obsession with perfection had begun years earlier, in Catholic school, where "the word came up every day. Every day, every deed had to be perfect. As early as high school I was a compulsive perfectionist about my work, and later I think I felt it was necessary because I was competing with my mother, who expected so much

Plumed Prayers, 1980

*Twenty-two-year-old Helen
helped her mother display her
paintings at a regional exhibition;
Helen was always conscious that
her mother "expected so much out
of [her] and so little from [her]."*

out of me and so little from me." By 1970, when Hardin's art was attracting independent attention, the competitiveness between the two was in full, poisonous flower, despite or perhaps in part because of Hardin's conviction that "people were going to buy my mom's things before they would buy mine." The salient exception had been the sojourn in Colombia, and now there would be another respite from rivalry: the U.S. cultural attaché in Bogota had talked to his counterpart in Guatemala City, and an invitation for a repetition of the Colombian triumph was forthcoming.

When Hardin wrote excitedly to inform her father, now back in Washington, D.C., of her good fortune, he responded with a letter asking if she could stall the consulate for another six months; he would be coming to Guatemala in 1971, he said, and they could be together. The necessary arrangements were made; the show, which contained a good deal of nontraditional material, came off well; and Hardin came home. *Song in the Sky* (1972), painted after her return, was representative of the clarity and control she brought to her best work in that period, but it did not reveal the circumstances under which it was created, for once again the creative conditions paramount in the studio were absent elsewhere. "I was working feverishly, drinking ten to fifteen cups of coffee a day, everything I was doing was art, art, art, I even ignored Margarete, I would get up at eight and work until two in the morning, it was crazy." Notwithstanding the distance of more than a decade, Hardin's recitation in a

Sityatki Vision, 1980

1984 interview of events of the early seventies was as breathless as her life must have been; reliving the years was agonizing. Entering the living room of their Albuquerque home, husband Cradoc Bagshaw dispelled his wife's tension:

"Did she tell you how loose she was in those days?"

Hardin (defensively, but with a teary smile): "I was not loose, I needed company."

Bagshaw (professorially): "Did she tell you about the married cops and doctors?"

Hardin (emphatically): "That's not true! Only the doctors were married."

Joking aside, the phrase "it was crazy" was more than a figure of speech. One night in November 1972, at an arts-and-crafts fair, Hardin, who had been depressed for weeks and had been taking prescribed "mood elevators," drank a glass of white wine, began crying, was unable to stop—"It was like I had just shorted out"—and lost consciousness. She awoke hours later in a psychiatric hospital, the Bernalillo County Mental Health Center, to find a nurse holding out a cup; the first words she heard were, "Would you urinate in this, please?" Hardin was on the ward close to a month. "They let me out right before Christmas. I was terrified—even driving scared me to death. I continued therapy with a clinical psychologist for nine months. Later I could see why it happened. It was all the pressure of being tossed back and forth from my mom to Pat, the pressure of raising Margarete on my own, the pressure of having almost no social life, the pressure of working all the time, all the time. Pressure. It all closed in."

The early 1970s was a frantic period for Helen, one that ended with her collapse and hospitalization.

Heavenly Protector, 1981

Song in the Sky, 1972

EIGHT

Prayers Of A Harmonious Chorus

Prayers of a Harmonious Chorus, 1976

"You've always dreamed of living there," Lee Eisenberg wrote in *Esquire,* May 1981, "the great good place where everything is going to be different. You're too late for Aspen, and Key West is too crowded. But don't give up. We've asked around and checked the maps. There's still a chance you can make it to Santa Fe…the Right Place." When Hardin read the article, it was with peals of laughter, even though one of the people profiled as the epitome of Western class was her own Santa Fe dealer, Forrest Fenn: "I always said, I can't go to hell when I die because I've been there already. Santa Fe. If I hadn't been there with Cradoc, I would never have made it."

Hardin met Cradoc Bagshaw, a lanky, boyishly loud, acerbic, hockey-playing freelance photographer, an outdoorsy Alaskan-in-exile who specialized in Indian subjects and who loved computers like summer loves sun, in January of 1973, scant weeks after her release from the Bernalillo County Mental Health Center. She was squired to a party in Santa Fe by another photographer, Buddy Mays, who had snapped the *Albuquerque Tribune* picture of her reading *New Mexico Magazine* in the hospital, and her first reaction to Bagshaw was that he was an interesting guy, but not the answer to her prayers. She *had* been praying. "When I was in my depression period for three or four months, before and after the hospital, I was praying all the time, in my mind, for help. I knew God wouldn't send down bolts of lightning to give me what I needed, a decent man who didn't tell lies—all I wanted was Mr. Utopia—but I had to find some kind of resolution. All the men I met turned out to be liars. When Cradoc started telling me what he'd done, I thought, 'Oh boy, another one'—he was too young to have done all that stuff."

But it was true: Bagshaw had lived a life both peripatetic and creative, a Jack Kerouac-kind of life minus the self-destruction, and he was ready to settle down. Hardin told Margarete: "I've met someone, he's just the tallest man I've ever seen, and he has the biggest, bluest eyes!" Margarete was ten. "I thought, 'Oh, here it goes again.'

Mom always had boyfriends, some of them married. I couldn't pronounce Cradoc's name and at first I was scared of him. He took us to a restaurant in Santa Fe, the Three Cities of Spain—now it's very trendy and called the Pink Adobe—and I had cold soup. I'd never had that before. He told us all these stories. I didn't believe any of them. Pretty soon, he started moving things into our house. I thought they would move out again. Then my mom asked, 'What would you say if I was to get married to Cradoc?' I said, 'Okay.' She said, 'Good, because if you said no, I was going to punch your lights out.' We both laughed."

Although Bagshaw was the last in a not exactly miserly line of men, Hardin had been serious about only two of them, the photographer Buddy Mays and a physician, Erv Hinds—neither man wanted marriage, which Hardin, who sported a pretend wedding ring at times to "legitimatize" Margarete, desperately desired. Bagshaw had no idea at their first meeting that he had been introduced to his future wife. "I didn't think she was beautiful and I didn't really like her art. I thought it was artsy-craftsy. Then my father came for a visit and saw it and was impressed. He told her she should be getting ten to twenty times what she was getting. No joking. There would come a year at Indian Market when I was carting stuff from the car to Helen's booth, and it all sold on the way to the booth, or just after it got set up there. I went back to get the rest of the paintings and some guy followed me and wanted to buy one. By the time I got to the booth again, Helen had sold everything I was bringing, sight unseen, on the basis of what was already there. But that was later, after I had come around, and fallen in love."

On July 3, 1973, Hardin became Mrs. Cradoc Bagshaw and the couple, along with Margarete, whom Bagshaw officially adopted, moved to Tesuque, a small town outside Santa Fe. "Moving Helen to Santa Fe," he reminisced with black but entirely affectionate humor some years after her death, "was like moving a mountain. She got depressed in Santa Fe and 'weirded out.' Then I moved her back to Albuquerque and she died. She didn't take to moving well."

Hardin was immediately popular with the Santa Fe artistic community, but it was an unenviable renown. "It must be so easy for you," a male Anglo artist confided, "Indian, and a woman, too." Worse than the condescending assumption that Hardin's success could be attributed to tokenism—she was one of the few living painters, and the only Indian female, to be carried by Fenn Galleries, a pretentious establishment specializing in pricey figurative art for the uncritically affluent—was the equally common and condescending assumption that she was a Noble Savage.

"The first thing whites from the East would say to me was, 'Oh, I really admire the American Indian. The American Indian has been put through so much, but you have so much dignity!' I would think to myself, 'They're not talking to me.' There are a lot of Indians who have been put through a lot, but I'm not one of them. As far as I know, what's put me through a lot is…life. The elders at Santa Clara put their own people through a lot; if you want change, you have to leave. I think that some of the pueblo's alcoholism can be partly explained by the frustration caused by the elders keeping everything so clamped down. It's hard on everyone. There are a lot of attitudes toward women in the pueblo, for instance, that are tribal, but there's a lot of plain old modern chauvinism, too." These were not sentiments that the deliciously guilt-ridden Anglo readers of *Bury My Heart At Wounded Knee,* or the wealthy collectors who snapped up each new Scholder canvas of a colorfully imploding Indian, wanted to hear; these were not sentiments apt to warm the heart of the hostess who invited Hardin to a soirée and then added, "All the Indian guests are going to come in traditional clothing. Would you mind?"

Patronization on the one hand, prejudice on the other: for the first time in her life, Hardin did learn in Santa Fe what it meant to be dismissed because she was an Indian. Peering at her checkbook, with its "Contemporary Indian Art" slogan under the name, a girl in a supermarket said, "So, you own a gallery?" Hardin told her no, she was an Indian artist. "Oh, I didn't think you were Indian," the girl said, "because Indians are too dumb to have checkbooks." At an art show, there was an argument with a security guard; when Bagshaw arrived to investigate, the officer had an order for him: "Control your wife."

Bagshaw (barely able to suppress his laughter): "Helen, I'm surprised, you know better than to talk that way to a man with a gun, your own father is a policeman."

Hardin: "I know, but he's not an asshole."

Hardin could redeem the incident by turning it into an anecdote, but her tenure on the board of directors of Santa Fe's huge outdoor art exhibition, Indian Market, was another matter—she was appointed, she thought, as a token, and then was pointedly ignored.

"The general attitude toward Indians in Santa Fe was to treat us like pets: be nice, stay in the corner and keep quiet. An Indian who could live in Disneyland could live in Santa Fe. The biggest disagreement I had with the Indian Market board was over posters and greeting cards, which sounds petty, but the artists wanted to be allowed to sell them, because they can be your bread and butter, and of course they are a way for people who couldn't afford the images otherwise to have them. The board thought nothing should be sold that had not been handmade by the Indians themselves. They allowed etchings, but not posters; my mom couldn't sell her Christmas cards. Well, they would have passed out if they'd known that a Hispanic guy with Anglo assistants printed all my etchings: they knew so little about art, let alone Indians, they thought I did them myself. I wrote them a letter of protest they never had the courtesy to answer."

Meanwhile, Hardin, Bagshaw and Margarete were building a house of their own, the Santa Fe dream. The trio went everywhere together—"fused at the hip," Bagshaw quipped—and although the interdependence would one day be seen as a liability, as something to grow out of, it acted as an effective bulwark against the stresses of Santa Fe. Hardin was still painting obsessively (she was providing the financial support for the housing venture while her husband provided the labor) when Bagshaw sat down with her to talk about pricing. "You shouldn't be doing *anything* for less than $100," he said. "Minimum. This $50 thing should stop. Look, Helen, the phone never stops ringing—there are people *in line* to buy paintings." She agreed and raised her prices between January and June 1974 by a third. "I took *Robes of Ghosts,* which appeared in a special *Arizona Highways* issue, into Margarete Chase," Hardin said. "I told her it would have to sell for $850. I thought she was going to faint. I started to get a little irritated with the Chases."

Velarde was in turn becoming irritated with Hardin and her husband: "Fred and Margarete took us under their wings and protected us from downfalls that we might have had and supported us pretty nicely. I love them both. Cradoc is very Anglo, he's a white man, if you ask me, he has no use for the low class. Poor Cradoc. I shouldn't say bad things about him." Her characteristic method of signalling and disguising aggression, her giggle, punctuated every sentence. "He's a nice guy, but he thinks in a high-toned level and I'm just a humble Indian. He's in a world where it's always mechanical and faster moving, whereas my world is just slow, you know, a walk-space. I think like an Indian, he thinks like a white man, never the twain shall meet."

And what did she think her daughter thought? "Ask Helen. She's progressive and aggressive. I think Cradoc's had a lot of influence on her. She gets mad at me because my work's cheap. Well, I said, I got nobody to support but me. Nowadays, I'm not pushing, Fred and Margarete are not pushing, we've all slowed down, and we're just here, like old monuments. I'm painting because I got nothing better to do. My home's paid for, my car's paid for, I'm eligible for Social Security, so what the heck? I'm content." Neither Hardin nor Bagshaw disputed Velarde's contentment, but both felt she had replaced the loss of two families—the tribal and the nuclear—with the paternalism of the Chases. (Bagshaw put the matter bluntly: "Pablita was content to pretend she was back on the reservation, doing piece work for the white man.") Each side in the dispute did acknowledge that changing times and shifting cultures were culpable in many cases for the misunderstandings and grievances: a portrait of Velarde that incorporated her children and her children's children would have to be entitled *Incantations of Relative Strangers.*

Exposure to art and artists in Santa Fe provoked in Hardin a twofold response. Her imagery became more daring, but her style was no less meticulous; if anything, it became more so. Fellow artists confronted with a painting such as *Lost Fertility Regained* (1974), with its clinically layered lines and its shriekingly sexual imagery, would take Hardin aside and ask, "How can you stand to do it? The work! So much time and energy on one painting." Hardin was surprised by the question. Her answer was always a simple, "You stick with it." But it was more complicated than that and she knew it. "Maybe," she theorized, "it's partly the woman in me, able to sit there and do the job until it's done. I'd see my mom work for hours, so to me it was no big deal. To me, studio time was never an hour or two, or an afternoon, it was all day, it was my job. It's funny. I told my mom I couldn't stand her earth pigments because they were too slow and there were too many layers. Now I'm doing the same thing in acrylics."

As the investment boom in Indian art that began in the late sixties—and continued until the 1981 bust—entrenched itself in Santa Fe, Hardin had an additional reason for pursuing perfection: it was her means of distinguishing herself from what she saw as the opportunism of so much commercially motivated Indian production. "I judged the 33rd Indian Art Annual Exhibition at the Philbrook in 1978 and I couldn't believe the crap." Bagshaw's influence was also important. "Until my mom met Cradoc, she was sometimes afraid of standing up for what she believed in," Margarete said. "That was one of the reasons she had her breakdown. He gave her confidence, just by demonstrating his own personal growth and change. My grandmother's right: he keeps moving along. Cradoc took Mom to Yellowstone on their honeymoon and it opened her eyes. The more she was exposed to, the more she wanted to be exposed to. And she really grew. You could see it in her art."

Her professional growth was not greeted with enthusiasm by her dealers. Fred Chase, squeamish about the overt sexuality of *Lost Fertility,* retitled the piece *Primitive Mural.* Another painting, a totem pole of overlapping heads, was equipped with the cutline *Masks After Picasso* (1976) when it popped up in *Arizona Highways.* "I would never call anything that," Hardin hooted. "I guess that was their bid for respectability: see, Picasso was primitive, too. He was lucky. I'm an Indian and he was a Spaniard but no one ever went around calling him a Spanish artist, as if that explained everything about him." By any title, *Masks After Picasso* (it had actually been sold untitled, a rare occurrence for Hardin) was a mediocre installment in another series, this one inspired by the winter dances at Santa Clara.

"They are dances for blessing in the new year. The men dance in such a way to wake the earth up. There are long, long lines of men moving their feet up and down, always in one place, chanting prayers. It's hypnotic. If you don't know the language, it sounds like they're singing the same thing over and over, but if you understand, the seasons are changing, the clouds are changing, the song is changing. All the men have been joined together, all the prayers have been joined together, the sounds and the voices have been joined together and become one thing. It's so much magic." Hardin's treatment of the sensation aroused by the dances ranged from her modest 1983 etching, *Unity of Prayers and Song,* with three singers, to the ambitious 1976 high point of the series, *Prayers of a Harmonious Chorus,* with ten heads melded into one.

"Everything may change in our demoralized world except the heart, man's love, and striving to know the divine. Painting, like all poetry, has its part in the divine," Marc Chagall wrote. It was an approach to art Hardin endorsed. But how to achieve the divine? For many mystics, rapture must be reached by the abdication of conscious control; for Hardin, the exact opposite was often true, and she saw no contradiction in becoming a prophetess of the compass, a sage of the ruler, a high priestess of the protractor. "I actually failed geometry in high school because I had no time for the theories, I was having too much fun with the designs. I love structure, ritual, patterns—that's one of the reasons I love the Catholic Church—and so I had to love geometry. In my senior year in high school the nuns told me I had had too much art, but I protested and the dean of girls said she would let me study art while the boys took drafting—we had boys' and girls' classes in our school. Out of the corner of my eye, I saw everything those boys did, I saw what they were using and how. I gave the gadgets a try, then put them away. It didn't sink in until years later, when I took them out again. Now, there are times when I am inspired by the shapes of the tools themselves. *Acoma Birds* (1977), which is just a little painting of two birds who have become friends, came about as much from the curves of my tools as from anything made by the Indians at Acoma Pueblo."

The attraction to geometry was virtually ancestral—throughout her childhood, Hardin was exposed at home to anthropology texts containing the work of the Hohokam, Mogollon and Anasazi peoples. The last, considered to be her own biological forebears, were divided by archaeologists into four developmental phases. The first two, Pueblo I and II, lasted until about A.D. 1050, when the decoration of pottery was believed to have begun in earnest. Pueblo III, A.D. 1050 to 1300, also known as the Classic Anasazi period, brought with it the cliff houses of Mesa Verde in Colorado and Canyon de Chelly in Arizona; pottery found at those sites and at Chaco Canyon and Kayenta is ornamented with interlocking shapes frequently filled by tiny parallel lines. Pueblo IV, which ended in 1700 with the establishment of Spanish hegemony in the Southwest, was an aesthetic efflorescence for the Anasazi—the austere geometry of Pueblo III gave way at Sikyatki and Awatobi to representations of recognizable but magnificently stylized kachinas, eagles and the like, and at Kuaua, Awatobi and other locales to the murals that captivated the imaginations of the students at The Studio. The Hohokam, whose modern descendents are probably the Pima, Tohono O'odham (Papago) and Yumans ("Hohokam" is a Pima term meaning "those who have gone"), inhabited the low desert country of southern Arizona from approximately A.D. 300 to 1400; they left behind handball courts and irrigation canals but because they cremated their dead, relatively little is known about them. Their pottery was exceptional for what Charles Avery Amsden characterized "the extemporaneous stroke." In comparing the Anasazi and the Hohokam, Amsden pointed out the Hohokam artist used "her brush in truly creative delineation, whereas the Pueblo decorator used hers as a methodical generator of prim lines in formal geometric figures. The

Acoma Birds, 1977

latter is a well-schooled draftsman, the former is an unschooled artist." Hardin combined in her finest Hohokam paintings the best of both worlds. *Hohokam Serenade* (1983) is a silvery haiku, a touchingly romantic moondance in which Kokopelli, the Bearer of Seeds, the flute-playing fertility god sometimes depicted with an erection, serenades a pregnant woman under a night sky; only the thinnest of blue-green lines penned around the pair departs from the black-and-white scheme—but this is a black-and-white scheme in which the blacks are glossy, the off-whites iridescent and the silvers crystalline. *Shadows of the Desert* (1984) adds to Kokopelli and his woman a figure symbolic of old age and a worker. The Hohokam pottery designs sprayed mistily on the marbleized background (prepared with a sponge) continue into the pedestal supporting the quartet, and by virtue of sharp outlining, the background thus becomes, ingeniously, the foreground. The figures are bas-reliefs modelled with acrylic paste and textured by running a No. 2 black lead pencil shallowly into their surface. Both paintings are ghostly evocations of shadowy spirits — *The Shadows of Our Forgotten Ancestors,* to borrow the title of a film by Sergei Paradjanov.

The Mogollon lived in southwestern New Mexico and parts of Arizona from 300 B.C. to A.D. 1450—one of their favorite humanoids was the "hocker" motif, a man with arms and legs akimbo, found in an extraordinary number of otherwise disparate cultures from Borneo to Brazil, from China to Costa Rica. (Hardin's version, *Mogollon Man,* 1982, places the froglike creature atop a geyser of geometry and all but spews him out of the picture space.) The Mogollon were mountain people, but a branch of Mogollon stock in southern New Mexico lived in the lowlands, along the Rio Mimbres, so named by the Spanish after the willows that grew along its banks. The Mimbreños left a graphic legacy unequalled in the Americas: in the bottoms of bowls that had been decorated around the rims with borders of Anasazi geometry, the Mimbreños crafted a veritable menagerie of insects, rabbits, frogs, dogs, lizards, turkeys, bees and countless other beasties. Hardin's passion for the iconography was keen, but in most cases intellectual rather than emotional.

Shadows of the Desert, 1984

"Before I do a major painting, I warm up. That's when I do my small Mimbres paintings, what I call my Mimbres potboilers," she said. "I do the background—spraying or painting or using a sponge—then I paint over the center for contrast, then I do the outlines with a pen, then I paint, and spray, and paint, over and over, until I get the effect I want, then I cover the whole thing with a polymer varnish that heightens the colors. It's a mechanical but enjoyable process. With a major painting, I usually begin with the image in my head—I don't do sketches or other kinds of preliminaries—and set out to put it down. To me, that's the real art, and the Mimbres stuff, while nice, is a way to get going."

The Mimbres paintings are distinguished by their technical dexterity, electrifyingly saturated color and unassuming wit. They are whimsical, decorative and enchanting; they were intended to be modest and they are. But there exist several other Mimbres-based works of larger ambition, "a way," as Hardin saw them, "to make the Mimbres series art." The monochrome *Dreams of a Mimbres Fisherman* (1982), with its liquid line arching, riverlike, over a huge fish and down around a fisherman, is a meditation on placidity and fluidity that can be contrasted with *Mimbres Rabbit Ceremonies* (1983), in which the rabbit vignettes are contained in circles that are in turn contained in ratchety borders that whirl, like unmatched cogs, in opposite directions, a shrewd representation of the hectic, scattered life of any rabbit, prehistoric or otherwise. *Mimbres Gathering* (1983), the most formal of the Mimbres storytelling paintings—the symmetry is total—is an intriguingly pagan rendition of Adam and Eve. Kokopelli's bag bulges with fertility, while his pregnant pre-Columbian Eve, mother of life, carries home an ithyphallic antelope. But the masterpiece of the series is doubtless the early *Mimbres Life Cycle* (1975), in which figures from four different bowls have been expertly organized into a mural with all the mystic grandeur of Kuaua, or of certain Christian triptychs: the graphic genius of the Mimbres craftsmen has been employed to express Hardin's deeply idealistic spirituality. (Kandinsky: "Form, even if it is quite abstract and geometrical, has an inward clang; it is a spiritual being with

Dreams of a Mimbres Fisherman, 1982

effects that coincide absolutely with that form.") Culley's analysis of *Mimbres Life Cycle* is cognizant of Hardin's spiritualization of design:

"The three large circles behind the figures establish the major divisions of the composition and are also a subtle reference to the origin of the figures. The adult stage of life and the importance of achieving a balance between man's spiritual and physical natures is emphasized by the fact that the smaller circle within the large center circle becomes the visual focal point of the composition. This is reinforced by the rhyming of the smaller circle in front of each of the two central figures and by the concentration of warm colors in this area. The figures of the shaman, the warrior-hunter and death each have a negative counterpart. The woman giving birth has no such counterpart but, interestingly enough, the negative image of the shadow of the figure representing the spiritual side of man overlaps her figure."

Hardin was pursuing not only technical perfection, but its spiritual concomitant—her art was a record of her involvement with a universe in which man was depicted, in Aristotle's phrase, "as he might and ought to be," a vision simultaneously Aristotelian and Jungian. She had no sympathy for what Kay Larson termed the twentieth century's "rage for disorder," and in that sense—as in many others—she was profoundly alienated from the artistic mainstream. It was an alienation that her years in Santa Fe taught her to accept, and even to celebrate.

Mimbres Rabbit Ceremonies, 1983

ABOVE: *Mimbres Life Cycle,* 1975

LEFT: *Mimbres Gathering,* 1983

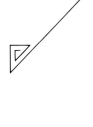

NINE

I Was Always On The Outside Looking In

When California art dealer Sue Di Maio visited Hardin at her Canyon Road studio in Santa Fe in 1979, it was with a mission: she had long admired her client's work, but she feared the pace the artist set for herself could not be maintained, and she hoped to persuade her to supplement her acrylics with carefully restricted printmaking. "I felt she had immense talent, but that she was in bondage to what she was doing," Di Maio explained. "I didn't see how she could keep up the standard of the originals indefinitely—she simply couldn't produce those wonderful paintings fast enough."

The offer to make prints had come to Hardin before, as early as 1972, but she had always demurred. "I wasn't ready yet," she shrugged. "I wasn't even happy with my painting." She was especially leery of lithography because she thought the lithographs of Gorman and Scholder were vastly inferior to their paintings, and she did not know, so spotty had her art education been, that there might be media more suitable to her sensibility and technique. Di Maio felt the "linear quality" of the work would adapt superlatively to etching and told her so; Hardin agreed, albeit unenthusiastically, to speak to Richard Ximenez, a master printer producing impeccably crafted editions for other artists at his El Cerro Graphics studio in Los Lunas, a few miles south of Albuquerque.

Messengers of the Sun,
print, 1980

"Richard and Helen hit it off right away," Di Maio reported, but Hardin's memory of the meeting was somewhat more complicated. She went into the conversation with Ximenez knowing only that her beloved Hohokam had etched sea shells; she did not know, for example, that colored etchings were feasible. "Richard talked to me about two hours and I didn't understand a word he said," Hardin laughed. "Then he wrote me a letter, a fat thing that must have taken three stamps to mail. So of course I thought, 'I've got to do etchings for this poor guy, he's gone to all this trouble.' What I didn't know is that etching is much more difficult than lithography. I found out. But I also found out that Sue was right: etching suited me perfectly."

123

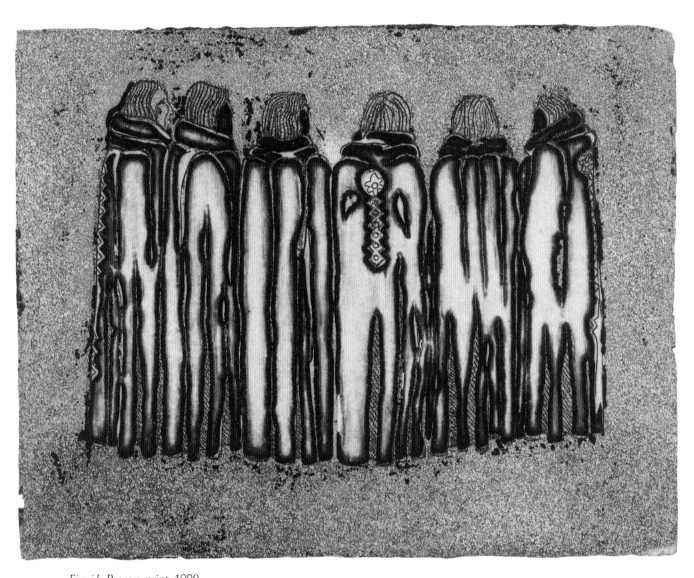

Fireside Prayers, print, 1980

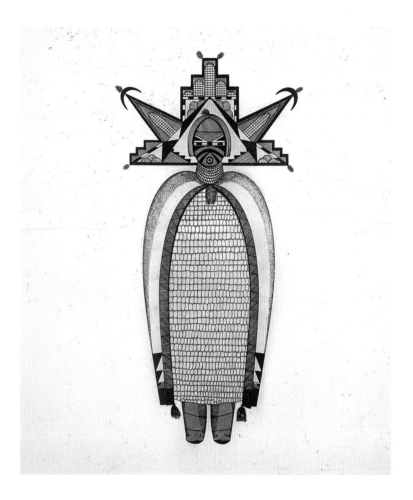

Bountiful Mother, print, 1980

By May of 1980, Hardin had produced four prints—*Fireside Prayers, Bountiful Mother, The Healers, Messenger of the Sun*—and it seemed appropriate that *Fireside Prayers* should have been first: the robed figures gathered in a smokey semicircle evoked *Medicine Talk* (1964) and *Chief's Robes* (1968), paintings that were benchmarks in her career. *The Healers,* a depiction of fetish bears thought to have medicinal properties, was a *homage* to traditional Indian iconography, as was the somewhat later *Deerslayer's Dream* (1981), which mystically married hunter to hunted by providing both with a "heart line," a symbol of eternal life rarely found in representations of human beings. *Messenger of the Sun* was a further exploration of the eagle, and *Bountiful Mother,* the most dramatic and perhaps the strongest of the initial prints, also had a rich resonance.

Deerslayer's Dream, print, 1981

Corn is the foundation of Hopi and Pueblo agriculture, and therefore of Hopi and Pueblo life—it is to the agrarian Indian of the Southwest what the buffalo was to the Indian of the Plains, and it has been accorded a similar degree of veneration. (When Pablita Velarde failed to find consolation in the teachings of the Catholic Church, she scattered cornmeal in her backyard, a ceremony whose origins are lost in antiquity.) The Plains Indian believed the spirit of the slain buffalo lived on in those who consumed his flesh; for the Pueblo Indian, the corn plant, an ever-present concretization of the kindness of creation, was "a living entity with a body similar to man's in many respects…the people built its flesh into their own. Hence corn was also their mother. Thus they knew their mother in two aspects which were often synonymous—as Mother Earth and the Corn Mother." (Frank Waters, *Book of the Hopi*.)

Hardin's *Bountiful Mother,* crowned by an angularly masculine *tablita* studded with phallic corn skyscrapers, dressed in a snowy feminine robe parted in a subtle vaginal oval across the pale blue corn kernels that make up the body, is ripe with fertility, *bursting* with it— she is as convincing in the amplitude of her fecundity as the 15,000-year-old Venus of Willendorf, grandmother of all such goddesses. Hardin had painted blue corn mothers before (a strain of blue corn is a Southwestern staple) and a favorite rendition, *Prayers of a Blue Corn Mother* (1974), completed not long after her move to Santa Fe, became a personal talisman, one of the few works, along with *Chief's Robes,* that she would not consider selling. Like *Chief's Robes, Prayers of a Blue Corn Mother* was initially rejected by her collectors— "People told me the eyes looked too Oriental, but because Indians are a Mongoloid race many of them do look like that"—and Hardin and her husband reacted by defensively investing the picture with the status of the proverbial last dime: as long as they owned it, they reasoned, they would never go broke. Another corn mother, *Morning Brings the Abundant Gift of Life* (1978), an overwhelmingly striking study set during what the Hopi call *Qöyangnuptu,* the first of the four phases of dawn, left Hardin weak with pleasure when she finished it: "She drove me wild, I loved her so much."

Morning Brings the Abundant Gift of Life was the centerpiece of one of the artist's more important shows in Santa Fe, an exhibition organized for the frankly extraordinary Forrest Fenn. *Esquire's* "The Right Place" article reported approvingly that "Fenn positively gleams when called a maverick" and described him as "a guy who strolls into the saloon with a Frederic Remington holster…audacious, outspoken, ever intriguing, Fenn stands in welcome contrast to the laid-back courtesies of old Santa Fe." (The "laid-back courtesies of old Santa Fe," a tri-cultural town whose Hispanic, Indian and Anglo populations existed, then and now, in an atmosphere bristling with racial tension, was an *Esquire* invention.) Asked by the author to discuss Hardin's art in 1983, Fenn said, "Helen is the most important Indian woman artist, but she can't be prolific enough. R.C. Gorman has made a ton of money but he's not the type to get very valuable; he's graceful and simple, but Fritz Scholder's work could be worth a lot sometime, hundreds of thousands of dollars. You can't predict it." At the height of the Indian art boom—the generally accepted theory is that the market crashed because inflation went down and interest rates went up, making investments in tangibles less attractive—Fenn revealed he cleared $375,000 in *one weekend* during Indian Market, but added that Indian art was for the most part a lousy investment: "If you bought a pot by Maria Martinez, the most famous Indian artist who ever lived, in 1925, your money would be worth more today if you'd put it in a savings account. There are some good investments in art, but if you buy [the works of] most Indian artists, you buy them because you like them." The idea of buying paintings "because you like them" seemed to strike Fenn as an odd but harmless eccentricity, one that, fortuitously, happened to be good for business.

The thoroughly commercialized attitude toward painting and sculpture implicit in Fenn's remarks was the rule rather than the exception in Santa Fe—the art of art elicited not much more respect in New Mexico's stunningly beautiful capital city, all narrow streets and flat-roofed adobes and art galleries (about one hundred of them), than the art of movies elicited in Hollywood, another company town only too ready to belittle its *raison d'etre.*

Prayers of a Blue Corn Mother, 1974

Morning Brings the Abundant Gift of Life, 1978

"Forrest always mentioned my 'inconsistent' pricing policies. He thought, as most dealers do, that paintings should be priced by size," Hardin said. "I priced by quality—a smaller one might cost more if I thought it was better than a larger one, where the composition was off, or whatever. Forrest never understood that. He asked me once if I wanted to be rich, famous or the best, and I told him the best. He said, 'Nonsense, you want to be all three.'" In pursuit of any or all of those ends, Hardin found that she faced another handicap, a triple whammy: that she was young, that she was attractive, that she was female. "That I was *Indian* helped sales," she reminisced caustically, "but that I was a woman held them back." She recalled sitting near a painting while a woman rhapsodized over it. "This," the woman said to Hardin, "must have been painted by an old Hopi medicine-man, it's got such magic in it." A flattered Hardin informed the woman that she was the artist; the woman, visibly dumbfounded, muttered a hasty, "It's very nice," and left—"You could see the 'magic' leak right out of it," Hardin chuckled good-naturedly.

"I have always lost sales to older women, if I stayed around so they could see I was not an 'old Hopi medicineman.' I never lost sales to older knowledgeable women, or to young professional women—especially single women, for some reason—but older wealthy women who are basically accessories to their husbands seem to be very intimidated by me. Their husbands would sometimes look at my art and like it, but not the wives." Hardin's frankness was an additional drawback in a town where Indians were expected to be noble and wise, but retiring and malleable. That her candor elicited disapproval in some quarters did not disturb her. "It's more important, finally, for people to like my art than to like me," she mused. "I would be just as happy if people said, 'Oh, she's a bitch, but I love her stuff.' That would not make me unhappy. I don't care if they think I'm a bitch. As long as they like my art."

In August of 1980, having become comfortable with and excited by the possibilities of etchings—"At first, I thought I would only do small things, to fill in, but some of them became as important as paintings, and I saw the best of them could stand on their own"—

Hardin began work on a new image, a bust developed from two earlier paintings, *Looking Within Myself I am Many Parts* (1976), and *Lady at Night* (1978). Both were unusual in that neither was presented frontally—in each, there was a slight Cubist suggestion of a profile. The severe, formal frontality of Hardin's art was her method of communing with the kachinas she painted, she said. "When I'm painting them, I'm being direct with them, and they have to be direct with me, so they have to face front." Her willingness to relax that imperative in the examples at hand may have been because both paintings were in some sense self-portraits, she decided, women who were looking both inward and outward, anxious to understand and harmonize their roles in two worlds. In 1976, when the Public Broadcasting System chose Hardin as the lone female painter in a series of documentary half-hours on Indian artists—also included were Scholder, Gorman, the Hopi jeweler Charles Loloma, the Apache sculptor Allan Houser, and the Pueblo potters Grace Medicine Flower and Joseph Lonewolf—she told the PBS film-makers that she wanted her program to "look healthy and whole." In the body of the documentary itself, which visited her studio, followed her to Puyé Cliffs and contained brief footage of her family, she returned again and again to her belief that life is a circle and that integration is paramount. "This is a circle that spirals inside itself," she said, as she drew a diagram in the dust with a stick for the camera. "That's how my life goes. This circle spirals and has new parts and someday will be complete but is not complete yet. The happier I am, the better my painting is, the happier my family is, it goes in a big circle." The poetry composed by James McGrath for the film expressed the same theme:

> *I travel upon the heart line of*
> *past and present, weaving in the*
> *sun pollen of who I am today,*
> *wading in the rain puddles*
> *of having too much to say because*
> *I must always speak from four directions.*

Looking Within Myself I am Many Parts, 1976

During filming of a PBS special at Puyé Cliffs in 1976, an introspective Helen Hardin reflected on her roles as mother and artist, and on the part her heritage played in her life and art.

Lady at Night, 1978

Her holistic impulses were thwarted by Santa Fe. She became increasingly unhappy in "the city different," as did her family, and when the move to Albuquerque was finally and joyfully made in late 1980, and she began *Metamorphosis,* she thought of the painting as "an angry woman getting out of Santa Fe and becoming a happy woman in Albuquerque. I hated Santa Fe so much that even to this day it makes me ill to think about it. When my mom would take me to the pueblo, or when I was living there as a very little girl, I was allowed to look at the dances but I never was allowed to participate. I was always on the outside looking in. Santa Fe was the same. I tried to join things so I could get into the community but everywhere I went, I felt I was still on the edge, that I was never going to integrate. I've never felt that way in Albuquerque."

The title Hardin chose for what would be her most ambitious etching to date was *Changing Woman* (1981)—*Metamorphosis* was completed immediately after the Albuquerque move, *Changing Woman* immediately before. The decorative aspects of *Lady at Night* vanished. (Hardin had commenced that painting as pure abstraction and did not add the face until she exhausted the design possibilities and asked Bagshaw what he thought she should do with the piece; he playfully turned it upside down and, pointing, said, "Why don't you put a face there?" She did.) Also missing is the intense Fauve palette of *Looking Within Myself,* which otherwise closely prefigured *Changing Woman* in its final form. When the proofs had been pulled,

it was obvious that Hardin had achieved a great synthesis, a powerful self-portrait: the artist as young woman and ageless kachina. The geometry that sometimes dominated her work was now utterly subservient to an underlying emotion. But what emotion? *Changing Woman* is an ambivalent woman, a woman in dissonant flux, a woman whose internal movements have been externalized by all those irregular, collapsing rectangles. No firm conclusions are possible as to her state of mind—happy? sad? in-between?—but her well-being or lack of it would prove to be a topic of a heated interpretive dispute wherever she was exhibited.

The etching superficially shared a Cubist goal, the desire to depict several surfaces simultaneously, but Hardin was not concerned with recording the conjunctions of physical planes. Her target was rather the multifaceted presentation of psychological levels, and what she achieved was nothing less than a portrait of the maelstrom within the mind: *Changing Woman* is a map of the psyche, the vaporous interior realm where thought and emotion fall weightlessly and vertiginously, tumbling out of an unknown past into an unknowable future. The image is not only or even a portrait of a woman, it is a blueprint of identity, and of identity seen as a product of mercurial and perhaps uncontrollable psychic processes *forever* in transition; in the guise of a female kachina, *Changing Woman* is a dizzying diagram of that same spiral of life Hardin had drawn in the dirt with her stick for PBS. "The years have transformed my blood," Nobel laureate Czeslaw Milosz wrote, "and thousands of planetary systems have been born and died in my flesh."

Hardin was so pleased with the etching she reproduced it in somewhat brighter hues as a painting (*Changing Woman*, 1981) that became a poster for the Babe Didrickson Memorial Golf Tournaments, conducted to benefit the American Cancer Society, but she did not at first plan to embark on a series. "I have always liked the idea of working in series, though, and when *Changing Woman* turned out so well I decided to go ahead. Exactly a year later, I did *Medicine Woman,* and almost exactly a year after that, *Listening Woman.* I thought for a while that I would conclude with *Winter Woman,* but

Changing Woman, four-color etching, 1981

then I decided I didn't want something symbolic of the end of life, and that I should do *Creative Woman* instead. That way, I kept it a series about professional women. For me, these are professional people, smart people. It's funny that woman collectors who are psychologists tend to buy *Listening Woman,* and doctors tend to like *Medicine Woman,* even if they don't know the titles. I thought that in other series of women I had seen by Indian artists—Gorman has been doing his women series for years and years—the emphasis had always been on the body, on the hands, on the boobs, on the feet, and everything was usually massive and masculine. I felt women are not that way, or at least not only that way. Women are also intellectual and emotional and sensitive, and that's what I wanted my series to be about—an intellectual series. My women do not have big boobs. (Or if they do, you don't see them.) My women have big brains. They are *all* brain."

Medicine Woman was derived from a 1980 kachina painting, *Arrival of Winter Messengers,* and *Listening Woman* from 1982's *Evergreen Kachina.* In both instances, focussing in close-up on the features simplified and strengthened the heads, and in both there is an added dimension: having been humanized and personalized, the women have become the repositories of a unique and unsettling combination of active anguish and covert ecstasy, *Medicine Woman* because the face is literally split in two, and *Listening Woman* because she appears, head hunched into her shoulders and eyes downturned, to have absorbed the sorrows of the universe. The emblematic heads are not negative or pessimistic—they are too solid in their self-sufficiency for that—but they are icons of the constancy of change, the timelessness of grief and the virtue of endurance. They are hymns to stoicism. The colors in all three—muted ochre, mustard, burnt umber, faded tangerine, bleached turquoise and charcoal—are masterfully orchestrated and harmonized; the emphasis is not on surfaces, but on interiors and essences. "Nothing is less real than realism," Georgia O'Keeffe argued. "It is only by selection, by elimination, by emphasis, that we get at the real meaning of things." The Hardin "Women Series" does get at the real meaning of things—at

Evergreen Kachina, 1982

the agony that accompanies change, at the hurt that accompanies healing, at the pain that accompanies empathy, and paradoxically, at the liberation that accompanies change, at the health that accompanies healing, at the knowledge that accompanies understanding.

"By now," Margarete commented, "my mom had developed her own Indian religion. She was Catholic, too, but she once told our priest that she didn't understand why she couldn't think of Jesus as someone she could ride her bike around the block with—she didn't really think of him as a deity, but as a friend. That blew the priest's mind. The way she looked at Jesus was very Indian, it was very Mimbres, from what we know about them; for Mom, Jesus was almost like another kachina. I think *Changing Woman, Listening Woman* and *Medicine Woman* were her real deities. All the knowledge she had accumulated, everything she got out of her life, she put into those three women. Now that she's dead, they're hard for me to look at."

In the spring of 1984, another departure: an overtly erotic etching, *Mimbres Kokopelli,* that shocked many of Hardin's collectors and dealers, despite the figure's whimsical, gentle nature. There is a wealth of sexually explicit Mimbres material, but little of it is disseminated in the textbooks used in university art and anthropology courses, and traditional Studio Indian art is, in any event, neuter as stone. "Look at this," Hardin said one afternoon, hoisting a huge tome, "see this picture of this bowl? All the other bowls are taken so you can see what's in the bottom. This bowl is taken from the side." Decorated in classic Mimbres style with a geometric border, the bowl was indeed coyly tipped; the portion of the composition visible was an innocuous but somehow incomplete line of figures. "What you don't see," Hardin smiled, "because the publishers have hidden it from the camera, is what the people are watching: a sex act."

Lost Fertility Regained, with its hermaphroditic totem, a reworked version of an image found at the Anasazi archaeological site Bidahochi, had embarrassed some viewers, and Hardin had eschewed any further sexual iconography; nonetheless, she knew that sexual imagery was a significant part of the heritage she consid-

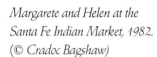

Margarete and Helen at the
Santa Fe Indian Market, 1982.
(© Cradoc Bagshaw)

ered her own. "There's a lot of sexual stuff I'd like to do, if I had about twelve hours to live," she joked. "My reluctance was because some dealers discouraged me to the point where I thought they might be right, that it might not be 'in good taste.' But you could do a whole series — you could do a whole prehistoric Indian sex show!" Perusing a preliminary sketch of *Mimbres Kokopelli,* she grinned. "He's a starry-eyed old man, holding on to his huge hard-on. He's probably surprised that he managed it. We're both surprised, he and I; I'm surprised that I went ahead and did what I wanted to do. In some ways, it's nice to have nothing to lose."

TEN
Harmony Brings Gifts From The Gods

About the time Hardin was completing the final phase of *Medicine Woman,* her doctor reported that a biopsy taken of a lump in her breast indicated the growth was malignant and a mastectomy would have to be scheduled. "I finished *Medicine Woman* just before he told me," she said matter-of-factly. "It was almost as if I needed that person, that healing spirit. After I found out I had cancer, and we were doing the print at El Cerro, I felt I had her spirit with me." The surgery took place in October of 1981, at a time when Hardin's career was at its most active, and she was pleased by the relative lack of trauma occasioned by the operation.

"Cradoc and I were very happy in Albuquerque. It was my biggest year in terms of sales and exhibitions—this was the last year of the Indian art boom—and I was everywhere, in Los Angeles, Denver, Tucson, Aspen, you name it. I read all these books about women having mastectomies, about their feelings of mutilation. It didn't cross my mind that I would feel like that. All I thought about was getting rid of the cancer. Maybe it was because I was a fat child. I never considered myself beautiful or any kind of sex object. I knew that in the eyes of whites, and some Indians, I looked better than other Indian girls—the short and *really* fat ones—and I know I am attractive to some extent, but I didn't see what all the fuss was about when people would go gaga and tell my mother how beautiful I was supposed to be. It just didn't phase me to lose that part of my body. Maybe I wasn't 'in like' with myself enough. Cradoc, who loves to make me feel better by saying outrageous things, told a friend of ours, when we were all talking about it, 'Well, if her boobs had been bigger…' That was his way of letting me know he would love me no matter what, even if there was nothing left of me but my brain, like one of the women in my series. I didn't feel less a woman. I just wanted to be healthy. For a while, I was."

The following spring, Hardin was hard at work on *Listening Woman* and was feeling fine. ("*Listening Woman* is the woman I am

Medicine Woman, four-color etching, 1981

143

only becoming now," she said in the spring of 1984. "She's the speaker, she's the person who's more objective, the listener and the compassionate person.")The mastectomy had been dealt with so successfully that when set upon by a particularly pushy Casanova at a party, she mischievously fantasized pulling her false breast out of her blouse and tossing it at her tormentor with, "Here—go in the corner and play with this." The printing of *Listening Woman* began in May of 1982, but by July, despite her doctors' reassurances, she knew she was unwell: "They all had the attitude that I was making a big deal out of nothing, that it was a clean mastectomy, mopped up with radiation, no problem. They told me they would do a bone scan, to make me feel better. The next day, one of the doctors said, 'I just looked at your X-rays and I'm afraid you do have some problem in your sternum.' He meant that the cancer had metastasized. The first thought I had was, 'Oh, my God, I haven't got all my work done, I'm not ready to die!' I could see one painting after another flashing in front of my eyes. Literally. It was like a slideshow. There I am, lying in the hospital bed, with these acrylic visions going through my head. I just kept thinking, 'I can't die, this is not true, this cannot be true.' Then Cradoc came in. The doctor had told him I also had tumors in my lungs—if the doctor told me that, I must have repressed it. I went from thinking it couldn't be true to thinking I wouldn't last longer than four months. I was very ignorant about cancer."

The prognosis was grave, yet, in the short run, promising: cancer of the type contracted by Hardin often responded well to chemotherapy. Her first, mild treatments resulted in a slight thinning of the hair, an insignificant loss in weight, and a ten-day period of ill health, similar to a bout of the flu. At the conclusion of the chemotherapy, her energy returned, the pain diminished, the tumors in the lungs disappeared and she dared hope the cure might be total. In the spring of 1983, there was a recurrence of the cancer in the lung, again treated satisfactorily with chemotherapy. By December of 1983, the tumor in the sternum, diagnosed as incurable but treatable, was subjected to pinpoint radiation, a process Hardin underwent while engaging in the majority of the interviews necessary to produce the

Listening Woman, four-color etching, 1982

present volume: she travelled to the clinic in the early morning, took a short nap at home, and then worked at reminiscing in the studio at the rear of the house, if she was feeling especially energetic, or in the living room, if she felt it advisable to rest on the couch.

"My doctor says it's incurable," she reiterated, "but he also says that I can stay well for periods of time. As things happen to me physically, I will be less and less able to deal with them; eventually, resistance just goes. So now cancer has become the Big Annoyance of my life, and I deal with it. I've had annoyances before—I could die tomorrow in a car wreck, driving to the hospital—and that's how I have to look at it. You know what's weird about people and their reaction to cancer? Most people don't know you can actually live with the disease. In my mind, it's sort of like being diabetic, and there are certain things you have to do to maintain your health. I take care of myself, I try to stay well. Being ill makes me think more about what I am going to do. I don't mess around, either with people or paintings."

Hardin had always had an eye on posterity: in her 1976 PBS special she confessed, with customary candor, "Many artists suffer from egomania and I'm one of them I guess. I have a great need to be remembered and I'll be remembered through my paintings. I have a great drive inside of me to be the best. I think the reason I don't fear death is because I know that I'll always be here through my paintings. I have a lifetime, no matter how long or how short, to do it in, and I want to be good at what I'm doing. I want to make it complete. It's the reward of living and the reward I have to give to those who survive me. It's the only thing I can give that's really me." Understandably, Bagshaw found the family's own videotape of the special nearly impossible to watch after his wife became ill: the documentary ends with Hardin vanishing into the summer air as she walks across a field near Puyé Cliffs. When the local PBS station, KNME-TV, sent an arts reporter, Hal Rhoades, to Hardin's home in 1983 to do a follow-up to the 1976 film, he found her sentiments little changed, although she did not accord to art the primacy she once had—"It's an important thing, but not the only thing." Rhoades asked if she would mind discussing her illness. "I haven't had cancer long," she said on camera. "At first I thought I was going to be all right, but I've had a recurrence and now I know I'm going to have a long struggle ahead of me. I'm not anxious about dying, but I feel a sense of relief, and I can't even describe it. It's almost as if a decision has been made for me that I didn't want to make a decision about." To the inevitable "How has it affected your art?," she said, "I'm freer. I'm doing things, now, the way I want to do them, the way I've *always* wanted to do them. I'm saying things now I've always wanted to say. Why not? What have I got to lose? I feel closer to myself, but I'm not withdrawn; I'm even more outgoing than I have been. I feel at the same time that I've really looked into myself."

The paintings of this period—the Hohokam studies *Shadows of the Desert* and *Hohokam Serenade*; the kachina trinity *Guardians of Infinity* (begun the day of the Rhoades interview), *Vision of Darkness, Mimbres Rabbit Ceremonies, Voices of Thunder*; and two masterpieces, *Harmony Brings Gifts from the Gods* (1982) and *Incantations of the Four Winds* (1983)—were by no means obvious departures. The images were more rigorously abstracted and the colors marginally bolder than in the bulk of the earlier work, but the craftsmanship was no less painstaking and the designs no less complex and inventive; the primary deviation was in scale, for these paintings were generally far larger than anything Hardin had attempted before. She found to her surprise that the bigger they became, the more appealing she found them. The monumental *Harmony Brings Gifts from the Gods,* which she gladly permitted the New Mexico Arts and Crafts Fair to reproduce as its 1983 poster, conjoined and climaxed the "harmonious chorus" series and the kachina series; it was a faultlessly assured composition provoked in part by an unexpected source, the prospect of the artist's first trip to New York. Hardin was to exhibit at Western Images, a gallery in Chester, New Jersey, owned by John and Judy Cacciola (Chester is the seat of "polo country," an affluent Manhattan bedroom community—the Marin County of the East—where local real estate contracts stipulate that fences must contain gaps to allow free access to horses during annual fox hunts) and she felt she should produce a painting that would, if only privately, commemorate the trip. "I thought of everything in New York as being side by side by side," she said. "So I thought of *Harmony Brings Gifts from the Gods* as…well, as *Kachinas Go to New York*. I was on a prescription pain medication while I was doing it, and I was relieved to find I could still paint, even if I was slightly stoned and a little out of control. I can't paint if I drink; after one beer or a glass of wine, I'm useless in the studio."

Where *Harmony Brings Gifts from the Gods* was both decorative and mystical, *Incantations of the Four Winds* was anecdotal, a nod toward narrative, but on a personal basis—Hardin never presumed the picture would impart to its viewers the precise meaning it held for her. "I thought of it as a storm weatherscape, a summer storm, where everything happens unpredictably. It's a great afternoon and ten minutes later thunderheads roll right over where you're having your picnic, the wind is blowing, the rain starts, and by the time you get your picnic back into the car, the sun's out again. That jagged line in the upper right corner is lightning, where it all begins."

Hardin's illness and her mother's decision to stop drinking solidified a tentative reconciliation commenced some years before. "She talks about her sickness, and is very frank about it," Pablita Velarde acknowledged in a whisper. "She's accepted the penalty of death coming at any time. I can't talk about it. I can't even talk about it with her. I only encourage her to work. Her work seems to help a lot—every time she feels good, she's painting. We've had problems. I won't deny it. When she was younger sometimes I think Helen put on a little bit of an air that didn't please me but other times she was so darn sweet she was truly my daughter. She wanted to advance with every step she took, whereas me, I just let time progress itself. All my life I never rushed. I used to tell Helen, 'time will take care of it, don't rush.'" Velarde sat motionless, her eyes without expression. "She had her reasons for rushing, after all. Now she's sick, and it makes me so mad that she had to go get sick like that, which isn't her fault." Her eyes filled with tears. "I blame God for that, to tell you the truth. I blame God."

Hohokam Serenade, 1983

Hardin did not. There was anger, to be sure. There were times when it was an ordeal to open an art book—when it hurt beyond articulation to see what a painter had been able to accomplish in an old age Hardin had little chance of reaching. There were times when the injustice was searing—when it was beyond toleration to think of brazenly self-destructive lives that lasted decades longer than Hardin's life was likely to last. There were times when the guilt was numbing, and those were some of the worst times, when Hardin would castigate herself for her past and would wonder aloud, "What was driving me? All along I wished I could have stopped and rested. Why didn't I? I didn't need to do all the things I did, I didn't need to paint all the paintings I painted, what was pushing me?—pushing, pushing, pushing. I thought I had it in balance, and…" And she would continue until sobs stilled her speech, until reality reasserted itself, until she could see that her depression had momentarily twisted her perceptions, and then she would laugh and say, "There: I'm turning it on myself again. Blaming myself for being sick. *That's* sick." And there were times when there was no pain, no anger, no resentment—there were times when she felt temperate and healthy and whole. "It's very strange," she said, "but I feel so at peace with myself, everything seems to be in balance, even though I'm physically falling apart."

Her relationship with the Church was close, a connection charged with warmth and relief. "I'm not frightened of God any more. There may have been a lot of good that came out of the discipline the nuns gave us, but they could have accomplished the same

Harmony Brings Gifts from the Gods, 1982

Incantations of the Four Winds, 1983

thing and more by speaking of God's love. For a long time, my relationship with the Catholic Church was on again, off again, like a bad marriage. What I loved was the sense of order, the incredible sense of history and beauty and art. And ritual: the structure of ritual ties the Church, for me, to the ceremonials of Indian religion. In Catholicism you're always preparing to meet the end and Indians go from day to day in sort of the same way. They don't live in the future, but they are always preparing, or staying prepared, I should say—on guard— for the end. If I were going to be an Indian all over again, I would ask God to make me a Pueblo Indian, because the rituals are largely intact. In Pueblo religions, the preparation is always for the next ceremonial; it's not real far ahead, just into the next season, but it's constant. A cycle. A circle. Always repeating. Going on." In the Mass performed at the Newman Center, a progressive Catholic parish on the campus of the University of New Mexico, Hardin found the comfort and contentment of the Pueblo ceremonial cycle. "The Mass is simple and musical. Occasionally they have a dud— sometimes they get a Franciscan guest in, and they're so stodgy and full of mildew it's like doing penance—but usually it's great, and it's wonderful to be participating in a ceremony I can love and feel good about the rest of the week."

Unsure of so much during her life, Hardin was by now certain of the meaning of her death. In December 1983, while she was preparing the paintings for the New York show, she took a break. A small Christmas tree was in the corner. Carols were issuing softly from a radio. Breaking a long period of silence, she said, "After I die, I think I'll go to heaven. I haven't robbed a bank or killed anyone, and I'm reasonably at peace with myself. All my life I thought of heaven as a place where Catholics go, because that's what I was taught as a child, that only Catholics go to heaven. They can't pull that on me any more. All good people go to heaven—wherever it is, whatever it is. They don't describe it any more as being with God and all the saints forever. They just sort of let it be a free place, where everybody is joined and happy. In the Pueblo religion, there is no supreme deity, a creator of all the kachinas—the universe is a shared responsibility.

It's almost as if there's a great pueblo in the sky, and in death it is as it is in life, except it's better in death, because in death, it's perpetual ceremonials. Maybe the heaven I go to will be like that, it'll be a Catholic heaven, but it'll be a big pueblo in the sky, too, where all the kachinas work together—a big world, somewhere else, where everything goes right, where everything is in harmony, and everything is perfect at last."

The trip to New York, which should by all rights have been the beginning for Hardin, was the beginning of the end. One afternoon she insisted on being taken through Central Park in a horse-drawn carriage. Bagshaw, knowing she was unwell and that the show was scheduled to open in a few days, attempted to postpone the adventure. "She insisted again," he said. "Now, I'm glad she did. As I was holding her in the carriage, I realized how fragile she had become—because of her illness, there had been little physical intimacy. It...hurt."

The next day, Hardin awoke in severe pain and was placed in a New Jersey hospital. Reviewing the results of the tests he had ordered, the attending physician told the couple there was a strong possibility the cancer had moved to the liver. Hardin and Bagshaw both knew that the diagnosis, if correct, meant death was mere months away. Hardin was too ill to attend her own opening; instead, she was presented with the preliminary manuscript of this book and waded through it, making notes, while Bagshaw appeared at the reception in her stead. She telephoned him halfway through. "The book is fine," she said, "though some factual things have to be changed." Then there was a long pause, followed by laughter. "It's a little like *Terms of* Indian *Endearment.* I guess that's been my life."

At home, the diagnosis was confirmed. She continued, when she could, to paint, and at her death left uncompleted her final image: *Last Dance of the Mimbres* (1984). The proofs for the erotic Mimbres etching were delivered during a particularly painful period and when Bagshaw asked what she wanted to title the print, Hardin sat up in bed, threw him a finger and said hoarsely, "Fuck you."

After he apologized for having bothered her, she managed a

Last Dance of the Mimbres, 1984

laugh and explained. "No, that's what I want to call it." She settled for *Mimbres Kokopelli.* The doctors told Bagshaw his wife might live for many months; she told him that she would not, that she thought she could, in the Indian manner, spiritually control the time of her death so as to avoid the worst of the pain.

The reactions of Hardin's family and friends to her illness had run the gamut from the support provided by her daughter Margarete—nineteen years old in 1984, and enrolled in a University of New Mexico pre-med program—to the abrupt emotional disengagement of several acquaintances. One friend called regularly to inform Hardin she was going to get well. "Finally I couldn't take the denial any longer and this is what I told her: 'There's something I have tried to say and you won't hear me. Please listen. I'm *not* going to be fine. I can't be cured, but I can stay alive for a while. I could stay alive until they find a cure for me, but in the meantime I could also get worse and die. I feel I have to tell you, because I want you to hear it from me, and not from someone else. I want you to know I'm doing my best. I want you to know I want to live. But there will come a time when everybody will have to kiss me goodbye.'" She was compelled to repeat that speech several times, for the benefit of other friends and relatives, but never for her husband. "I asked Cradoc one day, 'Do you mind if I die at home?' and he said, 'I would prefer it.' Cradoc and I do talk about it. The one thing he refuses to do is let me die. My aunt, Legoria, decided when she had cancer of the pancreas that after a certain point she would die, without going to the hospital for extraordinary measures, and she did; maybe that kind of control is an Indian thing. I know it's going to be real hard on Cradoc when I make my decision and say, 'I'm tired of this bullshit, I just want to go.' He'll fight it. But it is my decision, and I'm not afraid to die. I am afraid of pain. The only thing I pray for is that when the end comes, the tumor will go to my brain, because it'll be faster. It'll snuff out my life. The doctor says death is pain-free and comfortable. I hope so."

Hardin was correct in her fear that her family would not want to let her go. Bagshaw had long felt that his wife's reaction to cancer was unnecessarily fatalistic, although he admired her lack of denial. "Offered chemotherapy once more," he said, "she refused. 'What the hell difference would one more month make?' she asked me. After we came back from New York, it wasn't long before she was mostly bedridden and on morphine. She began letting go of things. 'You and Jay Scott will have to finish the book alone,' she told me. Someone requested an interview with her. She said yes, put on a wig and make-up and held forth, just like the old Helen, then collapsed in exhaustion the moment the interviewer left. Helen got angry at Margarete once, because Margarete also understandably had trouble letting her go: Helen sat up in bed, said, 'Well, here's my smile for today,' and lay back. Margarete was upset, but she also understood: it was hard for Helen to let herself leave when we were pulling for her to stay.

"She just let go of life, finally. The circle narrowed to the 'Women Series'—we'd put some of her work in her room—and to me and Margarete. Then she asked us to take her paintings and etchings out of her room. I think she didn't need to look at those faces any more because she was already there. She was with those people. She was one of them."

Helen Hardin died at home on June 9, 1984.

Helen was always insecure on earth. She was never sure of her place here. But she never doubted her place in the cosmos. I think she always knew she was O-Khoo-Wah. She was one of the Cloud People.

—JOHN NIETO

Afterword Return To The O-Khoo-Wah

Return of the Cloud People, 1972

She had asked to be cremated. The request horrified Pablita Velarde, who told Margarete, "I want to keep my Helen in one place, not blowing who knows where." Margarete tried to point out that the Hohokam had cremated their dead, and that the kind of burial Velarde wanted, the kind of burial she said was "traditional," was actually Christian, but to no avail. Velarde remained opposed to the cremation but resigned herself to the inevitable. The ashes—half of them—were scattered by Margarete and Bagshaw across Puyé Cliffs, the ancestral home where so much of Hardin's inspiration had been found and where she had so long ago been photographed vanishing into the sweet grass. The rest of the ashes were entrusted to Velarde for her "traditional" burial at Santa Clara Pueblo. "Thank you," Velarde said to Bagshaw when he handed her the urn, "even if these aren't my Helen's ashes." Telling the story more than a year later, in 1985, when she had quit school and was working at a gallery in Santa Fe, Margarete fought back tears. "Even in death," she said, "my mom was split in two."

By 1989, the wounds had healed. Bagshaw was pursuing his photographic career and was thinking of leaving Albuquerque. "There are too many ghosts here," he said. "Months ago, in a dream, Helen came to me, and I finally asked her to let me go."

Margarete married artist Greg Tindel, who had worked as a framer for Hardin, and is the proud mother of an infant daughter, named after Helen and nicknamed Birdie. "Over the years," Margarete said, "I've found myself talking a lot about Mom's death. She died with the dignity she wanted to have. Her death had so much to do with her life."

Acknowledgments

To Helen Hardin, of course — the achievement is hers, the faults are mine; Cradoc Bagshaw, Hardin's husband, and her daughter, Margarete Bagshaw Tindel, opened their homes and their hearts; Pablita Velarde opened the door to the painful past with courage and candor; Fred and Magarete Chase made their memories unstintingly available; Olivia Carabajal, Mary McClure and Liska Pepper were invaluable connections to the Southwest; Robert Houle, Gale Garnett, Hannah Fisher, Judith Milstein Katz, Wendy Burns and Ruth Gilbert were equally invaluable connections to Hardin's spirit; John and Judy Cacciola, and Sue Di Maio, were generous dealers; John and Renee Nieto were among the most discerning of her professional friends; Fritz Scholder was the most insightful of her professional "enemies"; Karen York, Ed O'Dacre, Les Buhasz, Shirley Sharzer, A. Roy Megarry and Norman Webster eased the pressure; JoAnne Dundas, Dan and Mary Corboy, Barry and Velma Cornish, Ernest Rivait, Rick Gallagher, Bruce Kirkland and Jennifer Stark, Joan and Dusty Cohl, John Coulbourn, Norman Jewison, Helga Stephenson, Trevor Gauvreau, Boaty Boatwright, Mary Scott and Heather MacGillivray each know why; Sallie Gouverneur and Susan McDonald made it reality.

Albuquerque/Toronto
1983-1989

Guardians of the Night, 1984

Robed Journey of the Rainbow Clan, 1976

Selected Bibliography

Adams, Clinton. *Fritz Scholder Lithographs.* Boston: New York Graphic Society, 1975.

Amsden, Charles Avery. *An Analysis of Hokokam Pottery Design.* Medallion Papers, No. 23, Gila Pueblo, Globe, Arizona, 1936.

Arnold, David L. "Pueblo Pottery: 2,000 Years of Artistry." *National Geographic,* November 1982.

Briggs, Walter. "Helen Hardin: Tsa-sah-wee-eh Does Her Thing." *New Mexico Magazine,* March/April 1970.

Broder, Patricia Janis. *The American West: The Modern Vision.* Boston, New York Graphic Society, 1984.

Brody, J. J. *Indian Painters and White Patrons.* Albuquerque: University of New Mexico Press, 1971.

Brown, Joseph Epes. *The Spirit of the American Indian.* Pendle Hill Pamphlet No. 136. Lebanon, Pennsylvania: Sowers Printing Co., 1964.

Canby, Thomas Y. "The Anasazi: Riddles of the Ruins." *National Geographic,* November 1982.

Coles, Robert. *Eskimos, Chicanos, Indians.* Vol. 4 of *Children of Crisis.* Boston: Atlantic Monthly Press/Little Brown and Co., 1977.

Cooper, Tom C., editor. "American Indian Art Series." *Arizona Highways* Special Issue, August 1976.

Covarrubias, Miguel. *The Eagle, the Jaguar, the Serpent: Indian Art of the Americas.* New York: Alfred A. Knopf, 1954.

Culley, LouAnn Farris. "Allegory and Metaphor in the Art of Helen Hardin." *Helicon Nine,* Fall 1981.

_____. "Helen Hardin: A Retrospective." *American Indian Art Magazine,* Summer 1979.

Dunn, Dorothy. *American Indian Painting of the Southwest and Plains Areas.* Albuquerque: University of New Mexico Press, 1968.

_____. Unpublished letter to Karen Shane, November 20, 1978.

Eisenberg, Lee. "The Right Place." *Esquire,* May 1981.

Enfield, Lisa Marie. "Santa Fe & Taos." *Diversion.* September 1981.

Exposition of Indian Tribal Arts, Inc. *Introduction to American Indian Art.* New York: Exposition of Indian Tribal Arts, Inc., 1931.

Feder, Norman. *American Indian Art.* New York: Harrison House/ Harry N. Abrams, 1982.

Fry, Jacqueline Delange. "Contemporary Arts in Non-western Societies." *artscanada,* vol. 28, no. 6, issue 162/163.

Hammond, Harmony, Lucy Lippard, Jaune Quick-to-See-Smith, and Erin Younger. *Women of Sweetgrass, Cedar and Sage.* New York: Gallery of the American Indian Community House, 1985.

Highwater, Jamake. *The Sweet Grass Lives On.* New York: Lippincott & Crowell, 1980.

Houle, Robert. "Alex Janvier: 20th Century Native Symbols and Images." *The Native Perspective,* vol. 2, no. 9, 1978.

————.*New Work by a New Generation.* Catalogue of the Norman Mackenzie Art Gallery, exhibition of July 9, 1982. Regina, Saskatchewan: University of Regina, 1982.

James, George Wharton. *New Mexico: Land of the Delight Makers.* Boston: The Page Co., 1920.

Jung, Carl G. *Man and His Symbols.* New York: Doubleday & Co., 1964.

Lacouture, Sheila. "Artist Helen Hardin Exhibit at CMM." *The Bernardsville [New Jersey] News,* October 7, 1982.

Larson, Kay. "Balthus the Baffler." *New York,* March 12, 1984.

LeBlanc, Steven A. *The Mimbres People: Ancient Pueblo Painters of the American Southwest.* New York: Thames and Hudson, Inc., 1983.

Lisle, Laurie. *Portrait of an Artist: A Biography of Georgia O'Keeffe.* New York: Seaview Books, 1980.

Merry, Edward S., editor. *Indian Life: The Magazine of the Inter-Tribal Indian Ceremonial,* August 1959.

Monthan, Guy and Doris. *Art and Indian Individualists.* Flagstaff: Northland Press, 1975.

Moulard, Barbara L. *Within the Underworld Sky: Mimbres Art in Context.* Pasadena, California: Twelvetrees Press, 1984.

Nelson, Mary Carroll. *Pabilita Velarde: The Story of an American Indian.* Minneapolis: Dillon Press, 1971.

Nichols, John. *The Nirvana Blues.* New York: Holt, Rinehart and Winston, 1981.

O'Connor, Patricia. "Becoming Creative Woman." *Albuquerque Living,* August 1984.

Richard, Paul. "Native Americana." *The Washington Post,* August 23, 1980.

Ryder, Kristina Marie. "In Search of Creative Woman: Helen Hardin, Santa Clara Pueblo Artist." Master's thesis, University of San Diego, 1986.

Scott, Jay. "From Out of the West: The Good, the Bad and the Worthless." *The [Toronto] Globe & Mail,* April 14, 1984.

———. "Helen Hardin's Subtle Revolt." *The [Toronto] Globe & Mail,* August 21, 1982.

———. " 'I Don't Know What Indian Art Is': Fritz Scholder Refutes His Reputation As the Genius Bad Boy of Indian Art." *The [Toronto] Globe & Mail,* May 11, 1985.

———. "I Lost It At the Trading Post." *Canadian Art,* Winter 1985.

Shane, Karen. "Helen Hardin (1943–1984): Casting Her Own Shadow." *Southwest Art,* June 1985.

Snodgrass-King, Jeanne. "In the Name of Progress: Is History Being Repeated?" *American Indian Art Magazine,* Spring 1985.

Spinden, Herbert Joseph, translator. *Songs of Tewa.* Santa Fe: Sunstone Press, 1976.

Spivey, Richard L. *Maria.* Flagstaff: Northland Press, 1979.

Stone, Ben. Unpublished letter to Karen Shane, October 16, 1978.

Tanner, Clara Lee. *Southwest Indian Painting.* Tucson: University of Arizona Press, 1973.

———. Unpublished letter to Karen Shane, [n.d.].

Taylor, Joshua C., William Peterson, R. Andrew Maas, and Rudy H. Turk. *Fritz Scholder.* New York: Rizzoli International, 1982.

Velarde, Pablita. *Old Father the Storyteller.* Globe, Arizona: Dale Stuart King, 1960.

Waters, Frank. *Book of the Hopi.* New York: Penguin Books, 1977.

Wentinck, Charles. *Modern and Primitive Art.* Oxford, England: Phaidon Press, Ltd., 1979.

Index to Art

EDITOR'S NOTE: *Helen Hardin worked predominantly in acrylic on board; when the art reproduced in this book is not in that medium, the appropriate medium is indicated. Further, due to the passage of time, insufficiency of records, and the nature of art collections, it has not been possible to ascertain specifics of size or ownership on most of the art reproduced in this volume. The publisher would appreciate being contacted by owners of Helen Hardin's work with these details so that, in future printings, this information can be included. Owners may write to Northland Publishing Company, P.O. Box 1389, Flagstaff, AZ 86002.*